REVELATION

AND

OTHER END TIME SCRIPTURES

God Bless Your Study

Jack Anderson

the late 1960s with the book *Things to Come* by Dwight Pentecost of Dallas Theological Seminary. Over the intervening years I was able to read several books on the subject and to hear several authorities, such as Bruce Dunn of First Presbyterian Church of Peoria, Illinois, at prophecy conferences in my church or in one of the area churches around our home in Wheaton, Illinois. It was not until the death of my wife in 1992 and my retirement that same year that I was able to concentrate on studies consisting largely of reading books and listening to tapes by such great leaders in the field as Dr. Walvoord, Dr. David Jeremiah, Dr. Ironside, Walter K. Price, Dr. Charles Ryrie, Hal Lindsey, Tim LaHaye, Billy Graham, David Larsen, David Breese, Dave Hunt, and many others. In 1998 I was requested to teach the book of Revelation to my small group at church. This required considerable concentrated study and an organized (or at least partially so) note system. After that teaching episode my daughter, who had been subject to some of the same kind of prophecy discussions during her youth and teen years as had I, requested that I formalize and type out my notes for the family to retain when I was gone. To think, she didn't seem to understand that we were all going to be raptured before I passed from the scene. Talk about *déjà vu*.

After several months of making excuses and thinking, "That's going to be a lot of work," at her insistence, I sat down and began to type out my notes. I realized almost immediately that my notes, in the form of a list of bullet points were not going to make much sense to anyone but me, and it had been five years since I had used my notes to study or teach and I wasn't sure I understood some of them. I could see my project expanding exponentially. The points had to be fleshed out and developed so now I was looking at a major expansion and additional study. The next two years were among the most enjoyable years of my life. My study seemed to be blessed by the Lord. When I would get stuck on the meaning of a passage or needed a supporting passage the Lord seemed to supply just what I needed. I'm sure that my previous studies influenced some of the interpretations reflected in this book, but I have been led to depart from the generally accepted interpretations of many of the passages and chapters. I do pray that the book reflects God's

PREFACE

From my earliest memories I recall Mother's interest in the "second coming." She had a tremendous interest in Bible study and prophecy in particular. This interest was promoted by a friend of the family who conducted a weekly women's Bible study in her home, during which time the ladies studied many subjects, but their favorite seemed to be prophecy, and Mother brought all these new ideas home for family discussion. Everyone used the Schofield Bible in those days, including the ladies, and were quite familiar with dispensationalism and the imminent return of the Lord. I am reasonably certain that Mother was convinced and had convinced Dad that the Rapture was sure to occur before either of them had to go meet Him in the normal way. During my teen years our church seemed to have an extraordinary number of prophecy conferences, and between Mother's enthusiasm and the visiting expositors I had the sinking feeling that I would not get out of high school before the Lord came again.

Well I made it—plus 60 years. During that time I developed my own personal interest in the study of prophecy. My ability to scratch that itch was, however, deferred for many years as I married a lovely lady, Virginia Schrock, raised four children, studied and passed the exam for Certified Public Accountant, focused on career goals and took graduate studies at the University of Chicago. I finally began a tentative study in

TABLE OF CONTENTS

This book is dedicated to:
Mother, Helen Garrett Anderson, who introduced me to prophecy
and Daughter, Cynthia R. Heslinga,
who encouraged me to write what I was talking about.

Pleasant Word (a division of WinePress Publishing, PO Box 428, Enumclaw, WA 98022) functions only as book publisher. As such, the ultimate design, content, editorial accuracy, and views expressed or implied in this work are those of the author.

ISBN 13: 978-1-4141-0983-1
ISBN 10: 1-4141-0983-0
Library of Congress Catalog Card Number: 2007901940

REVELATION

AND
OTHER END TIME SCRIPTURES

A NEW LOOK

JACK G. ANDERSON

Pleasant Word

truth and that He might use it for His glory and the understanding of many of that wonderful disclosure of our Savior, Christ Jesus, the book of Revelation.

—Jack Anderson

"Call to Me, and I will answer you, and I will tell you great and mighty things, which you do not know."

—Jeremiah 33:3

INTRODUCTION

The book of Revelation culminates in the second coming of Christ, which is one of the most often mentioned truths in the Bible—therefore making it one of the most important doctrines of Scripture. The second coming is mentioned 318 times in the 210 chapters of the New Testament. Acts 1:11 is the first time after Jesus' death and resurrection that His return is mentioned (and it is the first time the *way* He will return is expressed): "Jesus…will come in just the same way as you have watched Him go into heaven." The primary reason we study Revelation is largely because of its truth and disclosure about His return.

Revelation is primarily a disclosure of events of the last days of history immediately prior to the return of Christ. Human history will continue for a thousand years after Christ's return, but this will not be "history" as we know it today. As such, Revelation deals extensively with the tribulation and God's relationship with Israel and the earth during that time. It reveals God's anger, wrath, and the resulting judgment that He imposes on both Israel and the earth, but it also gives hope to those who have accepted Christ as Savior both before and after the judgment begins.

In the study of Revelation, most of the prophetic subjects (second coming of Christ, rapture, tribulation, antichrist, Babylon, millennium, and other lesser signs and subjects) will be considered, and there will be many references to the other books of the Bible. In fact, it is my opinion that Revelation can only be understood in light of the other Scriptures, particularly the Old Testament.

WHY AND HOW JESUS WILL RETURN

What are the reasons for Jesus' coming again? There appear to be three:

(1) To take the church to be with Him as His bride at the marriage supper of the Lamb—this is the "rapture phase" of His coming which is fulfilled in a quite different manner than the "second coming" phase, as we will learn later on.
(2) To restore Israel and deliver it from Satan and the antichrist.
(3) To claim David's throne and establish His kingdom and rule the earth for one thousand years prior to establishing the eternal kingdom.

What will be the signs of His coming? The disciples asked that very question in Matthew 24:3. (Note: As we will see later, all signs are of His second coming; there are no signs relative to the rapture.) Matthew 24 outlines several signs, including:

(1) "Many will come in My name"—false teachers and religious leaders—"and will mislead many" (24:5).
(2) "You will be hearing of wars and rumors of wars" (24:6).
(3) "They will deliver you to tribulation' "—Christians will be hated and subject to tribulation for their witness (24:9).
(4) "Many will fall away" (24:10).
(5) "Many false prophets will arise and mislead many" (24:11).
(6) "Lawlessness is increased" (24:12).
(7) "There will be a great tribulation" (24:21).

The tribulation will be an intense judgment of Israel and the world. Salvation will be available during the tribulation to those who had not heard the word prior to the beginning of the tribulation. Second Thessalonians 2:8-12 indicates that God will send a delusion to those who "did not receive the love of the truth so as to be saved" so that they "might believe what is false." According to verse 8, this is after the antichrist—the "lawless one"—is revealed (and although not mentioned in this passage, it is also after the rapture). This seems to refer to those who heard the way of salvation before the rapture and did not believe; they will be sent a delusion so they will not be able to believe after the tribulation period begins.

The tribulation will come to an end when, after seven years, Christ will return with His saints. After a final battle that results in Satan being chained for a thousand years, Christ will rule from the throne of David.

INTERPRETATION OF REVELATION

There are four basic approaches to the interpretation of Revelation:

1. Nonliteral, idealist, or allegorical

This interpretation considers Revelation to be merely a spiritual message, teaching that the book is one great allegory that should not be taken literally. This approach can lead to distorted views and artificial interpretations.

2. Preterist

This view considers Revelation to be symbolic history rather than prophecy; that is, John was writing about events taking place in his day. This view destroys any future significance of the book.

3. Historical

This interpretation considers Revelation to be a symbolic presentation of church history culminating in the second coming. This method was highly promoted by Reformation and nineteenth-century theologians such as Wycliffe, Luther, Isaac Newton, Whiston, Vitringa, Bengel, and Barnes. This position is now considered unsound because most of the book does not apply to the church.

4. Futurist

This interpretation considers Revelation to be futuristic beginning in chapter 4 and subject to future fulfillment. This allows a more literal interpretation of the book. In my view, this literal interpretation (which, of course, recognizes that certain passages are symbolic and treats them as such) is the most logical based upon what we know of other prophecies. For example, the prophecies in the Old Testament regarding the first coming of Christ (such as Isaiah 7:14; 9:6, and 53:1-12) were literally fulfilled. In addition, many other prophecies in practically every book of the Old Testament have been fulfilled literally and are verifiable from history. Why, then, should we believe that any other method of interpretation than a literal one should be used to understand Revelation? It is, then, from a futurist and literal perspective that we will proceed with the study of the book of Revelation.

KNOWING ABOUT JESUS' RETURN IS IMPORTANT

Prophecy is not there to tickle our spiritual and intellectual fancy; nor is it merely a mental exercise; instead, it comes with practical admonition. Many of the most dynamic Christians have been those interested and versed in the prophecies of Scripture. We need to be armed with knowledge of God's plans for the future, and that knowledge will have an influence on how we live today. There are many scriptural admonitions in this regard, some of which are listed below. All scriptural references are from the New American Standard translation. I have not included a transcript of the Scripture being discussed in all cases and would suggest you have a Bible available both for referencing the Revelation passages under discussion as well as other Bible passages to which I will refer.

(1) Live in anticipation of His coming and watch for signs.

Therefore be on the alert, for you do not know which day your Lord is coming...For this reason you be ready too; for the Son of Man is coming at an hour when you do not think He will.

—Matthew 24:42, 44

(2)   Refrain from judging. He will take care of that when He comes.

Therefore do not go on passing judgment before the time, but wait until the Lord comes.

—1 Corinthians 4:5

(3) Regularly, through Communion, proclaim your faith in the Lord's death and resurrection until He comes.

For as often as you eat this bread and drink the cup, you proclaim the Lord's death until He comes.

—1 Corinthians 11:26

(4) Conduct your life in holiness and avoid sins of passion, so that you will be revealed with Him at His return in glory.

When Christ, who is our life, is revealed, then you also will be revealed with Him in glory. Therefore consider the members of your earthly body as dead to immorality, impurity, passion, evil desire, and greed, which amounts to idolatry.

—Colossians 3:4-5

(5) Relate to others in love in order to be holy before Christ at His coming.

May the Lord cause you to increase and abound in love for one another, and for all men, just as we also do for you; so that He may establish your hearts unblamable in holiness before our God and Father at the coming of our Lord Jesus with all His saints.

—1 Thessalonians 3:12-13

(6) Preach, be ready at any time to admonish, but with patient instruction.

I solemnly charge you in the presence of God and of Christ Jesus, who is to judge the living and the dead, and by His appearing and His kingdom: preach the word; be ready in season and out of season; reprove, rebuke, exhort, with great patience and instruction.

—2 Timothy 4:1-2

Since this book is specifically addressed to Timothy, I believe these comments are largely applicable to pastors; however, they are proceeded in 2 Timothy 3 by comments regarding the events of the last days and the adequacy of the man of God, thereby making them applicable to all who are saved.

(7) Hold fast; do not waver; assemble and encourage others as you see the day—that is of the Lord's return—approaching.

Let us hold fast the confession of our hope without wavering, for He who promised is faithful; and let us consider how to stimulate one another to love and good deeds, not forsaking our own assembling together, as is the habit of some, but encouraging one another; and all the more, as you see the day drawing near.

—Hebrews 10:23-25

How can we see the day approaching if we have not become familiar with the signs and what we are to look for?

(8) Be patient.

Be patient, therefore, brethren, until the coming of the Lord…You too be patient; strengthen your hearts, for the coming of the Lord is at hand.

—James 5:7-8

(9) Be holy.

What sort of people ought you to be in holy conduct and godliness, looking for and hastening the coming of the day of God…Beloved, since you look for these things, be diligent to be found by Him in peace, spotless and blameless.

—2 Peter 3:11-12, 14

(10) To know Him now and live in His Word will result in your being comfortable in His presence at His return.

And now, little children, abide in Him, so that when He appears, we may have confidence and not shrink away from Him in shame at His coming.

—1 John 2:28

(11) If you believe He is coming, your life will show it.

Beloved, now we are children of God, and it has not appeared as yet what we shall be. We know that, when He appears, we shall be like Him, because we shall see Him just as He is. And everyone who has this hope fixed on Him purifies himself, just as He is pure.

—1 John 3:2-3

As these words of Scripture instruct us, our study of the prophecies relative to the end times will give us an awareness of the nearness of the Lord's coming. This awareness should motivate us to live more closely to Him as those days approach.

As we begin this study, we should make one major assumption—-the end times are close at hand. Most probably the Lord's return will take place before the current relationships and balance of power between the nations of the world change significantly. This assumption has a basis in reality and is not unreasonable due to the 1948 Treaty of Rome in which Israel was reestablished as a nation for the first time in over two thousand years This action began the process of opening the graves, putting life in the dry bones, and bringing them into the land of Israel, as prophesied in Ezekiel 37. The "graves" are the nations in which the Jewish people are exiled; the dry bones are the nation of Israel.

HISTORICAL POSITIONS

Authorship

Beginning with Dionysius in the third century, scholars have challenged the apostle John's authorship—mainly because the Greek dialect and language are not as accurate as they would expect of John. Many suggest that the author was John the Presbyter or John the Elder mentioned by Papias as preserved in the writings of Eusebius. Others suggest John Mark. We accept the apostle John as the author of Revelation. Historically, there is good support for this conclusion—Clement of Alexandria and Eusebius affirmed that John was on Patmos (as is mentioned in Revelation 1:9).

Date

There have been two schools of thought on the date—some believe Revelation was written in 68 or 69 A.D. because Papias said John was martyred before the destruction of Jerusalem in 70 A.D. Others say the book was written in 95 or 96 A.D. because Eusebius commented that John left Patmos following the death of Domitian in 96. The majority opinion leans to the 95 A.D. date of writing.

Inspiration/Canonicity

Revelation was slow in gaining universal recognition as Scripture. The early church generally accepted Revelation by the end of the second century, but some scholars (such as Luther, Zwingli, and Erasmus) considered it nonapostolic.

REVELATION 1

—◎◎◎—

Verses 1 and 2

These verses introduce us to the authority for the book. God (the One "who reveals mysteries," see Daniel 2:28-29) gave this Revelation to Jesus to show to His bond-servants (note the plural noun—so it is apparently to all who believe, including us), which He gave to an angel to reveal to John, His bond-servant. God thereby authorized the disclosure of all that is in the book, possibly expanding on Christ's comment in Matthew 24:36 that only the Father knows the day and the hour of His Son's return. This is the "Revelation of Jesus Christ." *Revelation* is a translation of the Greek word *apokalypsis* which means "revelation, disclosure, or unveiling"; it is a revelation, a disclosure, an unveiling of the truth about Christ. He is more than the humble Servant we knew from the Gospels; in Revelation we see His power and glory. The substance of the revelation is described as "things which must shortly take place." "Shortly," as used here, means that the events described will not necessarily take place soon, but that when they begin to take place they will come to pass rather quickly.

Verse 3

Verse 3 is of utmost importance to us—it promises a blessing to: (1) the one who reads, and (2) all who hear the words of the prophecy and heed the things which are written in it. This is the only book in the Bible that contains such a direct promise. It should also be noted that the participles are in the present tense, indicating that the reading, hearing, and heeding (observing) are to be continuous. The book of Revelation should be read and periodically reread to refresh personal understanding and keep the words of the prophecy in mind. Why such a blessing? The most logical reason is to encourage the reading and hearing the words of this book. I believe Satan hates the book because it describes Christ's victory and Satan's defeat; he will keep people from reading it by convincing them of the impossibility of interpretation. In my opinion we should be hearing from this book regularly in church, even if it is only the reading of a portion from time to time on a regular basis.

One other important disclosure in the preface is that Revelation is referred to as "the prophecy" implying that the book as a whole is prophetic. This, in itself, seems to discredit those interpretation theories that the book is merely allegorical, spiritual, or symbolic. It should also be noted that the interpretation of prophecy, in general, carries a special warning in 2 Peter 1:20-21: "But know this first of all, that no prophecy of Scripture is a matter of one's own interpretation, for no prophecy was ever made by an act of human will, but men moved by the Holy Spirit spoke from God."

Verse 4

Verse 4 informs the reader of those to whom the letter was addressed—seven churches in Asia. Why seven churches? Certainly not because there were no other churches; many more than seven churches existed at this time. It is possible that these seven churches represented all churches (that seems to be the most generally accepted guess). Based upon God's presentations of other matters and His use of visual aids to make a point, I believe that Jesus' words to these seven churches (and what each represented) gave Him the opportunity to speak directly to His church at large (present and future) and express His feelings about certain matters, both good and bad. Up to this point, He had not addressed His church directly, but only through the apostles. Here He addressed those matters He felt were important by using as examples representative churches that were having the problems and doing the good things He wanted to address.

Verses 5 and 6

John extends greetings from the "publishers," who are a rather profound group—"Him who is and who was and who is to come" (God the Father); "the seven spirits who are before His throne" (most probably the Holy Spirit, see Isaiah 11:1-2); "Jesus Christ" (the Son). The Son is ascribed three titles—"faithful witness, firstborn of the dead, and the ruler of the kings of the earth." Special emphasis is also given to what He has done for us—He loves us, He released us from our sins by His blood, and He made us kingdom priests to His God and Father (note God is also "His").

Verses 7 and 8

Verses 7 and 8 present the synopsis of the book—Christ will return (*parousia*) in the clouds and "every eye will see Him, even those who pierced Him." Most commentators attempt to understand this in relation to those who are alive on earth at the time of His return. They suggest various scenarios that would allow all on earth to see Him. I believe the statement clearly refers to everyone, both living and dead, who will all be aware of and will be able to "see" His glorious return. Matthew 24:30 refers to this event in much the same way, but that passage is preceded by interesting comments that may help to explain His visibility. His return will occur immediately after the tribulation at which time "the sun will be darkened, and the moon will not give its light, and the stars will fall from the sky, and the powers of the heavens will be shaken" (Matthew 24:29). Now these events would sure get everyone's attention—just as the appearance and His glory will be shining brilliantly against a dark sky. I don't believe He will need that kind of backdrop in order to be seen, but I do believe that this will be such a glorious and victorious event that everyone who has ever lived will see it from wherever they are. More on this when we get to it in our study.

This introductory section closes with a powerful statement of who He truly is—"the Alpha and the Omega" (the beginning and the end) "who is and who was and who is to come, the Almighty." The "Almighty" is the one the Jews expected as their Messiah (see Psalm 110; Jeremiah 23:5-6). That is why so many did not recognize Him when He came the first time as a humble servant. They were looking for a king.

Verses 9 through 11

Verses 9 through 11 lead us into an introduction to the author, the apostle John, as he identified with the churches to whom he had been instructed to write. He was a fellow believer who had been exiled to the island of Patmos. He was, of course, well known by these churches and he could truthfully say he was their "fellow partaker" in tribulation because he had been exiled by the Roman emperor Domitian and had to work in the mines on Patmos. Although at this time John was approximately 90 years old, he did not complain about his plight. It is notable that his experience paralleled that of many Old Testament prophets—Moses wrote the Pentateuch in the wilderness; David wrote many psalms while being pursued by Saul; Isaiah lived in difficult days and died a martyr's death; Ezekiel wrote in exile; Jeremiah's life was filled with trials and persecution; even Peter wrote his two letters shortly before he was martyred.

John says he was "in the Spirit on the Lord's Day." There is some disagreement as to what this phrase intended. Many believe it referred to Sunday, as it is used today, but if that is the case it would be the first time it was used that way in Scripture. On the other hand, many believe this referred to the "day of the Lord," a familiar reference in Scripture to an extended period of time at the end of the age in which God deals in judgment on and has sovereign rule over the earth; however, this would be the first time this period was phrased as "the Lord's Day." I believe the reference may have been even more profound than either of these interpretations. As we will see, John was interactive with the characters that he observes, indicating it was more than a vision but more of a "transport" of his Spirit through time or into another dimension—and he referred to that as "the Lord's Day." Whatever is meant makes no difference to John's message. He clearly has a vision of Jesus, beginning with the sound of a voice telling him to write what he sees in a book and send it to the seven named churches.

Verses 12 through 19

This section introduces us to the glorified Christ. John turned to see who was talking and saw one like a son of man standing in the middle of seven golden lampstands (reminding us of Matthew 18:20, "Where two or three have gathered together in My name, there am I in their midst"). In verse 20, these lampstands are identified as churches. The countenance of the man who was standing in the middle of the lampstands was brilliant, like the sun shining in its strength. We get glimpses of Christ in His glory throughout Scripture, but this is the only place we see Him in His entirety. In Matthew 17:2, we see Christ on the Mount of Transfiguration and His face "shone like the sun." In Isaiah 6:1, the train of His robe filled the temple. In Daniel 7:9, the Ancient of Days appeared and the hair on His head was like pure wool; here in Revelation, His hair is described as "white like white wool, like snow (verse 14). Some commentators believe that is a sign of purity, wisdom, and justice. This may be true, but I don't believe there is scriptural support for that assumption. His eyes are like a flame of fire; His vision is penetrating (verse 14). Hebrews 4:13 says, "There is no creature hidden from His sight, but all things are open and laid bare to the eyes of Him with whom we have to do." His feet were like burnished bronze and His voice like the sound of many waters (verse 15). This is much like Daniel's vision in Daniel 10:6. In His right hand (which always refers to authority and control, see Ephesians 1:20) He held seven stars (verse 16), which are identified in verse 20 as angels of the seven churches. Out of His mouth came words of great power ("sharp two-edged sword," as described in Hebrews 4:12 and Revelation 19:15, 21).

There is no mention of nail scars; this is not the meek and humble Servant. As noted, every eye shall see Him in His glory, as brilliant as the sun against a dark and fearful sky. As did others who were exposed to a vision of the Father or the Son, John fell on his face as if dead until the Lord laid a hand on him and said, "Do not be afraid." He went on to identify Himself with an astounding statement: "I am the first and the last, and the living One; and I was dead, and behold, I am alive forevermore, and I have the keys of death and of Hades."

He then tells John to write (1) "the things which you have seen," (2) "the things which are," and (3) the things which shall take place after these things" (verse 19). This is a key verse to understanding Revelation. The Lord identifies what He is going to reveal to John in His Revelation (see verse 1) and it includes three items. Most commentators agree that item 1 is reflected in chapter 1; item 2 is the messages to the seven churches reflected in chapters 2 and 3; and item 3 is reflected in the remaining chapters 4 through 21.

Verse 20

Verse 20 explains portions of the previous verses—the seven stars are angels of the seven churches, and the lampstands are the churches. The angels are messengers, and some believe they refer to those appointed by God to lead the local congregations.

REVELATION 2

Chapter 2 begins the second major division as outlined by Christ in 1:19, that is, "the things which are." There are many interpretations about what these churches represent. Some consider each of the churches as representing a particular time period of the church age and therefore these messages were prophetic in nature since these ages were yet to come when Christ gave these messages to John. The ages have been assigned to the various churches as follows: Ephesus (first-century church); Smyrna (second- and third-century persecuted church); Pergamum (312 to 500 A.D.); Thyatira (Dark ages to sixteenth century); Sardis (Renaissance and Reformation); Philadelphia (nineteenth-century revival); Laodicea—end time apostasy.

I do not feel that is the correct interpretation. I would agree, instead, with those who believe that each of these churches represents a different set of characteristics of church congregations that have existed since the earliest days of the church age and are existent in churches today as well. It seems to me that since these seven letters are the only direct communication of Christ to His bride, the church, the messages to these churches were intended to be for guidance of the conduct of the church during all ages as it tries to deal with these characteristics. These letters may be the most important message in Scripture for that purpose.

CHURCH AT EPHESUS

The first church to be addressed was in Ephesus. This city was a center of commerce, much of which was the manufacture and sale of idols for the worship of Diana—goddess of fertility. A temple of Diana (or Artemis, the Greek name for the Roman goddess) was located in that city. The temple was one of the seven wonders of the ancient world. The silversmiths who made and sold images of the idol were quite upset with Paul and others who were preaching the message of salvation in Jesus Christ in Ephesus and throughout Asia, convincing many that the worship of Artemis was useless. The preachers were ruining the business of the silversmiths because the more people who became believers, the fewer who would purchase the idol images. A silversmith named Demetrius incited a riot in Ephesus by condemning Paul (see Acts 19:24-41).

Verses 1-3

Most of the churches were addressed by Christ from the aspect of one of His attributes expressed in chapter 1. Ephesus was addressed by He who holds (controls) seven stars (angels of the seven churches) and who walks among the seven golden lampstands (seven churches). This was an important reminder that He was ever present and observed their work and also their attitude. He noted that the members of the church of Ephesus were patient, hard-working, not able to endure (put up with) evil. They tested those who called themselves apostles and found them to be false. These believers persevered for Christ's sake and had not grown tired.

Verse 4

Christ had one thing against them, however. They had "left" (note—not "lost") their first love. We are not told here what was meant by their "first love." Ephesians 1:15 may give us some idea, for there Paul wrote of having heard of their faith in the Lord and their love of the saints. If they had weakened in their faith and love of Christ, then they had probably left their love for all the saints and one another. A recent study of church growth proved that a growing church is more loving and caring than a static or declining church. Loving churches attract more people regardless of theology, denomination, or location. Love and acceptance seem to be the key to growth.

Verse 5

Verse 5 gives this church the formula for returning to Christ's standard—remember, repent, and do the deeds done before (loving one another). It is interesting to note that Christ did not ask them to pray or to get organized or to do anything other than get to work doing the thing that was common to them at an earlier time—love for Christ and one another. Paul had reminded them in Ephesians 2:8-10: "For by grace you have been saved through faith; and that not of yourselves, it is the gift of God; not as a result of works…For we are His workmanship, created in Christ Jesus for good works, which God prepared beforehand, that we should walk in them." In other words, works do not come before salvation, but salvation comes before works; God has already prepared works He wants done, so there apparently is no need to make up any on our own.

They were then told that He would remove the light (lampstand) of this church if they did not repent; removing the lampstand would mean that the church would no longer have influence in the world for Christ. Apparently they did not repent, and He did remove their lampstand, for this city and church eventually declined and disappeared.

Verse 6

This verse gives another bit of encouragement. This was an active, dynamic church with major pluses in the Lord's sight because they hated the deeds of the Nicolaitans, which the Lord also hated. The Nicolaitans were followers of Nicolaus of Antioch who later defected from the Christian faith through preaching non-Christian doctrine. He split the church by establishing a priesthood that ruled the laity. The Nicolaitans also advocated complete freedom in conduct, including heathen feasts and free love.

Verse 7

Jesus' final admonition to this, as well as to all the other churches, was, "He who has an ear, let him hear what the Spirit says to the churches." There is some uncertainty about the meaning of this phrase, but it seems first of all to focus the message to the church and the Gentiles. The Lord had used this phrase in Mark 4:9 as He was teaching the disciples in parables; in Mark 9:11-12 He then explained what it meant. He made it clear that He used parables so "those who are outside" could not understand His teaching about the mystery of the kingdom of God. He quoted from the prophet Isaiah. In Isaiah 6, Isaiah responded to the Lord's question, "Whom shall I send, and who will go for Us?" by saying, "Here am I. Send me!" Isaiah was immediately given the message, "Go, and tell this people: 'Keep on listening, but do not perceive; keep on looking, but do not understand.' Render the hearts of this people insensitive, their ears dull, and their eyes dim, lest they see with their eyes, hear with their ears, understand with their hearts, and return and be healed" (Isaiah 6:9-10). Isaiah asked how long this judgment would last, and the Lord replied that it would be in effect until cities were devastated, houses were without people, and the land was desolate. This may refer to when the time of the Gentiles is fulfilled, which we will touch on later.

We do know that during the time of Christ this judgment was still in effect, for in Matthew 13:14-15 Christ stated that Isaiah's prophecy was being fulfilled, and He quoted from Isaiah 6. Paul also indicated that this judgment was still in effect in Romans 11:7-8. It appears this judgment, issued in Isaiah's time, established the provision for the salvation of Gentiles hundreds of years later after Christ's death on the cross. It seems that the Lord established this judgment on Israel to harden their hearts, for if they had heard with their ears, understood with their hearts and returned to the Lord and accepted their Messiah, He would have had to heal them. This would not happen, for He had promised that "it is too small a thing that You should be My Servant to raise up the tribes of Jacob, and to restore the preserved ones of Israel; I will also make You a light of the nations so that My salvation may reach to the end of the earth" (Isaiah 49:6; see also Acts 13:47). Paul also referred to this judgment against Israel in Romans 11:8, "God gave them a spirit of stupor, eyes to see not and ears to hear not, down to this very day." Continuing on into verse 11, Paul picks up on the result of the judgment, "They did not stumble so as to fall, did they? May it never be! But by their transgression salvation has come to the Gentiles, to make them [the Jews] jealous." In Revelation, those who can hear are believers in these churches (mostly Gentiles) as opposed to those who cannot hear (Israel), thereby focusing the message and emphasizing it to the church.

The closing comment to Ephesus was a personal rather than a corporate message to the church. "Him who overcomes" presumably referred to those who applied the message. They would "eat of the tree of life, which is in the Paradise of God," a place first mentioned by Christ while on the cross when He promised the thief beside Him: "Today you shall be with Me in Paradise" (Luke 23:43).

Even though they were hardworking, patient, and unable to endure evil, Christ's major concern with the believers in Ephesus was that they had left their faith in Him and apparently their love of the saints, thereby losing their witness and light for Him in the world.

Church at Smyrna

The church at Smyrna is addressed in verses 8 through 11. It was a church going through considerable persecution—what would He say to such a suffering church? Smyrna was about thirty-five miles north of Ephesus. It had been established as a Greek colony in about 1000 B.C. on a huge hill called the Hill of Pagus. The city was destroyed in 600 B.C., then rebuilt by one of the four generals serving Alexander the Great in about 300 B.C. The inhabitants were proud that the city had "risen from the dead." Historians opined it as one of the most beautiful cities that the Greeks had built, one of the most beautiful in Asia. Smyrna was called the crown of Iconia and the ornament of Asia. It was a major source of myrrh, a sweet perfume used in embalming— "Smyrna" means myrrh. It was also the birthplace of Homer, the Greek poet who is thought to have written the *Iliad* and the *Odyssey*. Polycarp, bishop of Smyrna and one of the apostolic fathers of the church, was martyred in about 155

A.D. by being burned at the stake for his faith in Christ. The city exists yet today as Ismos in Turkey.

Verse 8

Smyrna was noted for its wickedness and opposition to Christianity. Christ addressed the church in this city as the "first and the last, who was dead, and has come to life"—a confrontation with their national pride of "rising from the dead" in rebuilding the city. Christ had a particularly unique relationship with Smyrna: He had received myrrh as a gift at His birth (Matthew 2:11), was anointed with myrrh at His death (John 19:39), and as a bridegroom was described as fragrant with myrrh, aloes, and cassia (Psalm 45:8).

Verse 9

The Christians of Smyrna lived in abject poverty and were disdained by the general population. They were tortured unbearably by many means—fed to lions, crucified, burned at the stake, and boiled in oil; they were denied work, and their homes were vandalized and robbed. The population was proud of being Roman and overly zealous about patriotism, ending up establishing emperor worship. Ultimately, this led to required worship of the emperor. Christ expressed His concern, saying, "I know your tribulation and your poverty," but He said, "you are rich." He also noted that part of their problem was those Jews who were Jews by birth but not by faith. They were being used by Satan to blaspheme the church just as they had been doing since Paul's time and were, as Christ expressed it, "a synagogue of Satan."

Verse 10

Christ had no condemnation for this church and only two instructions: "Do not fear what you are about to suffer" and "be faithful until death" Apparently some of them were to be thrown into prison at the devil's behest; they would suffer and be tested for ten days. This suffering may well have been to the death because many had been killed in various ways, as mentioned above. His promise was that those who were faithful unto death would receive the crown of life.

Verse 11

Apparently the persecutions were to continue and get worse. As mentioned above, Polycarp was the bishop in the church in Smyrna and ministered there for many years. He ultimately was asked to recant his faith in Christ and he replied, "Fourscore and six years have I served the Lord and He never wronged me. How then can I blaspheme my King and Savior?" He was burned at the stake in about 155 A.D. (less than a hundred years after John wrote Revelation). His primary antagonists were the Jews whom Christ had condemned as being those who said they were Jews but were not and were of the synagogue of Satan.

Jesus also promised that, as the Spirit says to the churches, those who overcome shall not be hurt by the "second death" (see 20:14). Just what you would like to hear if you were undergoing pressures—worried about family, no job, no income, being persecuted unto death—don't fear, be faithful. Well, that is the instruction the Lord gave to this church: Tie a knot in the rope called faith and hang on with both hands. The message is not to run or fight or compromise but to stand strong, steadfast, and faithful.

This instruction is applicable to the church today in many parts of the world as extreme persecution is inflicted upon many Christians. In Christ's view, they are rich.

CHURCH AT PERGAMUM

Verses 12 through 17 are directed to Pergamum, the most prominent city in Asia. It had been the capital of Asia for four hundred years and was the capital of the Roman government in Asia during the time Rome controlled that area. The most northern of the cities addressed by the Lord, it was wealthy. It had many temples devoted to idol worship and was an important religious center of the pagan cults of Athena, Asclepius, Dionysius, and Zeus. Asclepius, a god of medicine, was particularly identified with Pergamum. The idol was in the form of a snake—very probably the forerunner of the snake on a staff that is a symbol for the practice of medicine today. There was a university at Pergamum and its most famous treasure was a library of 200 thousand volumes, which was later sent to Egypt as a gift from Antony to Cleopatra. Its most important product was paper or parchment that apparently originated there and was called "pergamina."

Verses 12-13

Christ spoke to Pergamum as the one who had the sharp two-edged sword—a symbol of judgment. Just as He can create by His word (as noted in Psalm 33:6-9, which concludes, "For He spoke, and it was done"), He can also execute judgment by His word. It is not surprising that Christ addressed Pergamum from His position as judge for He knew they lived where Satan's throne was, and that Satan dwelt there. A "throne" implies a kingdom. Satan had apparently moved the seat of his kingdom from Babylon to Pergamum. From early times, Babylon had been considered the capital of Satan's kingdom. Idolatry started there through Nimrod and his wife Semiramis, but Babylon declined and was left desolate. Presumably Satan looked for another location and selected Pergamum because it was a focal point for many idolatrous religions.

As a leader in education, medicine, and pagan religion, Pergamum was an ideal environment for Satan to spread his evil religions. It is no wonder Christ viewed this location from the perspective of a judge. The Lord commended the church for holding fast to His name and not denying the faith even though they were engulfed in evil during the days of Antipas. According to tradition, Antipas (whom Christ here called "My witness, My faithful one, who was killed") was the first martyr in Asia, having been roasted to death during the reign of Diacletion.

Verse 14

The Lord had two complaints against the church in Pergamum, however. Some of their number held to the teaching of Balaam—eating things sacrificed to idols and committing sexual sins. As related in Numbers 22–25, Balaam taught that it was all right for the Israelites to intermarry with the heathen Midianite women. This resulted in idolatry as these women seduced the Israelite men into worshiping their gods, and God punished the Israelites with a plague. According to Numbers 31, Moses was so angry with his army captains who had allowed the Midianite women to live and intermarry with the Jewish men (which had aroused God's anger and caused the resulting plague), he ordered that all the women and their male offspring be killed. Undoubtedly there was a similar intermarriage and compromise situation going on in the church at Pergamum where civic and religious life were so intertwined. For instance, practically all meat in the town had been offered to idols before it was eaten; therefore, it was difficult to accept social engagements or even buy meat without some sense of compromise.

The apostle Paul wrote about this very problem of eating meat sacrificed to idols to the Corinthian believers. In 1 Corinthians 8, he used their liberty in Christ to explain that eating meat sacrificed to idols was not a sin for "we know that there is no such thing as an idol in the world, and that there is no God but one" (8:4). He continued in verse 7, "However not all men have this knowledge; but some, being accustomed to the idol until now, eat food as if it were sacrificed to an idol; and their conscience being weak is defiled." If someone with a weak conscience sees another believer eating food sacrificed to idols, he may be encouraged to do so. But since his conscience is not yet completely free, the guilt he feels ruins him. Thus, Paul points out to all believers that with freedom comes responsibility: "Therefore, if food causes my brother to stumble, I will never eat meat again, so that I might not cause my brother to stumble" (8:13).

Then Paul came back to the subject in 1 Corinthians 10 and expanded on his previous comments. Apparently he had further thoughts of even greater significance to the issue of eating meat that had been sacrificed in a pagan temple. He repeated the fact that an idol is nothing (10:19-20), but made the point that, in reality, the sacrifice to idols is the sacrifice to demons. Paul did not want the Corinthians to become sharers in demons. As he wrote in 10:23, "All things are lawful, but not all things are profitable. All things are lawful, but not all things edify." In 10:25-28, he modified his instructions to them by telling them that they need not question whether meat sold in the market or meat served by an unbeliever had been sacrificed to idols. However, if at any time they were told that the meat they were about to purchase or eat had been sacrificed to an idol, they should not buy it or eat it "for the sake of the one who informed you, and for conscience' sake."

Apparently in Pergamum, it was well known by everyone that nearly all meat had been sacrificed to idols, thereby rendering all meat inedible for the Christians. The actions of the church resulted in spiritual fornication in the union of the church and Satan's pagan religions. The believers compromised and were too tolerant.

Verses 15-17

As with the church at Ephesus, this church had some who followed the doctrine of the Nicolaitans, and as with Ephesus, the Lord expressed His disapproval. The Nicolaitan cult professed faith in Christ but taught a free love moral code. Here again the church was being tolerant and allowing some of its members to bring unacceptable doctrine into the church, presumably with the thought that it wouldn't hurt anything. Christ felt quite differently.

When believers compromise and tolerate all manner of evil, it soon becomes popular to be a Christian and the conscience of the church is quickly blurred. Christ has strong words for this attitude: "Repent therefore; or else I am coming to you quickly, and I will make war against them with the sword of My mouth." To him who overcomes, however, Christ will give hidden manna (Christ, as the bread of life), a white stone, and a new name written on that stone that no one knows except the one who receives it (referring to a special intimate relationship with Christ).

Apparently the church in Pergamum felt it had liberty in these matters, but Christ's condemnation of the doctrine of Balaam is clear testimony that Christians are expected to remain in right doctrine, separate from the world and its lax moral standards. The modern church has not done that, and the result is a blurred and uncertain testimony to the world. Today in many churches, it is difficult to distinguish between that church and the world. Biblical standards and doctrine are being compromised daily so believers can be considered "tolerant" and "non-judgmental." The church today would do well to take seriously the threat of compromise.

CHURCH AT THYATIRA

Thyatira, a small, thriving town about forty miles southeast of Pergamum, had been established as a Macedonian colony by Alexander the Great. It was famous for the manufacture of purple dye (which was really red) and for trade guilds which manufactured cloth. Thyatira is most familiar from its mention in Acts 16:14-15 as the home of Lydia, a seller of purple fabrics, and the place of her conversion. It is remarkable that Christ addressed this small church with such an important and severe message. This is also the longest of the seven messages. All was not well in Thyatira.

Verse 18

Christ described Himself to this church as "the Son of God, who has eyes like a flame of fire, and His feet are like burnished bronze." Here the speaker left no doubt who He was; this is the first and only time in Revelation that He uses the term "Son of God." There can be no doubt who we've been discussing. This is an interesting distinction between the description here and that in chapter 1, where He was called the "Son of man." Perhaps it was to reemphasize His two-fold nature, but possibly and more likely He is mentioned here as the Son of God because the Thyatirans worshiped the sun god and the church had become distracted. Their diversion in worship was so extreme that they had to be reminded who was speaking to and judging them. His eyes are brought to bear here as He says "I am He who searches the minds and hearts" (verse 23). His feet, like burnished bronze, symbolize His going forth to judge evil.

Verse 19

His commendation of the church at Thyatira is remarkable considering the condemnation to come. He mentioned their deeds, love, faith, service, and perseverance, and that their deeds had recently been greater than at first. None of the other churches were commended for love, without which, according to 1 Corinthians 13, nothing else is profitable. What more commendation could one want?

Verses 20-23

Christ had something against them, however. They had no discernment. They were laboring, loyal, and loving, but they did not know doctrine and didn't seem to care. A self-proclaimed prophetess named Jezebel had convinced some of the Lord's servants in the church at Thyatira that it was all right to eat things sacrificed to idols (see explanation about this under verse 14, church at Pergamum) and to commit fornication. To make matters worse, some manuscripts use "thy" before the word "woman" instead of "the" (in verse 20), indicating that she was a church leader in a dominant position (some interpret her to be the pastor's wife). She may have been named Jezebel, or was called that here because she was fulfilling the role of the historic Jezebel of the Old Testament who attempted to combine Israel's worship of God with the worship of Baal. So evil was the Old Testament Jezebel that she was singled out for a special prophecy that she would come to a sudden end and her body would be eaten by dogs (2 Kings 9:10, 30-37). She was the epitome of corruption and a symbol of immorality and idolatry. Christ took care of this Jezebel of Thyatira Himself by pronouncing a terrible judgment on her, her family, and those in the church who followed her. He gave her and those who followed her time to repent. She did not, so He gave her a sickness and killed her children with a pestilence. If any who followed her did not repent, He promised them a great tribulation.

Verses 24-25

Christ had a special word for those who had not listened to the teaching of Jezebel and who had not known the so-called deep things of Satan. The reference to the "deep things of Satan" appears to be a sarcastic remark—Satan's deep things are so superficial that anyone can understand them, whereas the "depths of God" can only be understood by the Holy Spirit (1 Corinthians 2:6-10). His special word to these people was that He would place no further burden on them other than holding fast to what they already had until He comes (this is the first time in the seven messages Christ refers to His coming). It is interesting to note that a similar message was sent with Paul and Barnabas to the Gentile believers in Antioch by the church at Jerusalem in Acts 15:28-29; that is, they would put no greater burden on the Christians in Antioch than for them to abstain from things sacrificed to idols and from fornication.

Verses 26-29

After this admonition, Christ promised the believers in Thyatira that those who overcame and kept His deeds until the end would have authority over nations and rule them with a rod of iron, for Jesus also has received authority from His Father (Psalm 2:7-9). He must, therefore expect these people to be with Him as He returns to earth at His second coming; Scripture says He will come back at the head of an army of those in heaven to rule the nations with a rod of iron (19:15). Jesus also promised the faithful ones Himself, as the morning star (see also 22:16). This star shines in a dark sky just before dawn, as will Christ at His coming (Matthew 24:29-30), just before the dawn of a new era.

Apparently the most significant problem at Thyatira was the lack of the teaching and study of sound doctrine with which those who were misled could have discerned the false doctrine of Jezebel. Many churches of today have fallen in the same way as Thyatira. They express love and emphasize doing good deeds, but they don't teach sound doctrine because they are either too busy or too concerned about being judgmental or intolerant. They ignore the instructions of Paul to Titus, that a church leader must always be "holding fast the faithful word which is in accordance with the teaching, that he may be able both to exhort in sound doctrine and to refute those who contradict" (Titus 1:9). Just as Jezebel led the bondservants of Christ astray in Thyatira, many today are espousing false doctrines that lead many astray. In 1 Timothy 4:1, Paul expressed this concern, "The Spirit explicitly says that in later times some will fall away from the faith, paying attention to deceitful spirits and doctrines of demons." He continued, "Prescribe and teach these things [referring to sound doctrine]…Give attention to the public reading of Scripture, to exhortation and teaching" (verses 11, 13). Without the teaching of sound doctrine and emphasis on study of the Word, doctrines of demons will flourish.

REVELATION 3

CHURCH AT SARDIS

Chapter 3 begins with a message to the church at Sardis. Sardis was at one time the capital of Lydia and was an important city on the trade route running east and west through that country. It had returned to prominence under Roman rule. Its wealth came from textile, dye, and jewelry. A magnificent temple of Artemis dating from the fourth century B.C. was located there and the ruins exist today in the small village of Sart, the remains of Sardis. The city practiced pagan worship and there were many mystery cults or secret religious societies. It was famed for its strategic location on Mount Tmolus and was considered to be impregnable; however, it had been captured by both King Cyrus of Persia and Antiochus III of Syria. The most famous king of Sardis was a man named Croesus who was extremely wealthy and the source of the saying "rich as Croesus."

Verses 1-3

Christ addressed this church as "He who has the seven Spirits of God," and from chapter 1, the "seven stars." The seven spirits speak to those qualities that insure righteous judgment. Isaiah indicated regarding Christ that the Spirit of the Lord would rest on Him, the spirit of wisdom, understanding, counsel, strength, knowledge, and fear of the Lord, "and He will not judge by what His eyes see, nor make a decision by what His ears hear; but with righteousness He will judge the poor, and decide with fairness for the afflicted of the earth; and He will strike the earth with the rod of His mouth, and with the breath of His lips He will slay the wicked" (Isaiah 11:2-4). The seven stars who are the angels of the seven churches He held in His right hand indicate that it is He to whom the leaders of the church are responsible, and to whom they will be accountable.

The church in Sardis had a good reputation and was considered a spiritual church among other churches. Christ saw through this false front, however. He knew their reputation as a spiritual church was not deserved for they were "dead." Sardis was surrounded by the grossest forms of idolatry. The pagan people worshiped the mother goddess Cybele. Sins of the foulest and darkest impurity were committed at festivals in her honor. The church was apparently full of nominal Christians who participated in the pagan festivals, for He indicated there were only a few who had "not soiled their garments" (verse 4). These few still had true life and spirituality, but the things they did do were incomplete. There was some possibility to strengthen what remained. He exhorted them to:

(1) *Wake up* and strengthen the things that remain, for He had not found their deeds completed in the sight of His God. Ephesians 2:10 says that we are created in Christ Jesus for good works which God prepared beforehand, that we should walk in them. Therefore, they should…

(2) *remember* what they had received and heard, which was probably the fundamental doctrine they had received as a young church,

(3) *keep* it, and

(4) *repent.*

Furthermore, He warned that if they did not wake up, He would come like a thief and they would not know at what hour He would come. It is interesting that this is the same symbolism as in 1 Thessalonians

5:4 regarding His second coming. He was not referring to His second coming here, but presumably He was referring to His coming to the church at Sardis and the resulting judgment that would accompany His coming. They would both be unexpected, sudden, and irrevocable.

Verses 4-6

The few godly were given a promise that they would walk with Christ in white (a symbol of purity), their names would not be erased from the book of life, and He would confess their names before His Father and before His angels. This statement has bothered some expositors who consider the book of life to be a register of those who have been saved and are citizens of the kingdom; to them, the statement conflicts with other Scriptures that indicate "once saved, always saved." Due to this discrepancy, it is now thought that the book of life is a registry of all births, and the names of those who do not accept Christ as Savior are blotted out.

Sardis was the only church that received no commendations; it was a dead church. It had probably died slowly over many years, member by member, compromising theology by theology, service by service, deed by deed, forgetting to watch and be alert to the compromises of basic doctrines of the faith. This is an example to the church today and an example of the care which Christ expects His church to display regarding His word.

CHURCH AT PHILADELPHIA

The church at Philadelphia was a faithful church to both Christ and the Word. The city known as Alaskia in modern times is located in Lydia twenty-eight miles southeast of Sardis. It was named after a king of Pergamum, Attalus Philadelphia, who built the city. The city was built on a mountain range and suffered through several earthquakes, one of which, in 17 A.D., destroyed the city, but it was rebuilt by Emperor Tiberius. It was a center of grape production and was also known for textiles and leather goods. During the time of the Roman Empire it was an Imperial Post due to its position on major highways and was known as the gateway to the east. Dionysius was one of the chief objects of pagan worship there. A nominal Christian testimony continued through the centuries even under Turkish rule. As is well known, Philadelphia means "brotherly love."

Verses 7-8

Christ is presented to Philadelphia differently than to all of the other churches, and the description does not coincide with any identifiers in chapter 1, other than the reference to having the key of David. In chapter 1, it is noted that Christ has the keys (plural) of death and Hades (1:18). The allusion here seems to be tied to Isaiah 22:22 where Eliakim had the key to all the treasure of the king and "when he opens no one will shut, when he shuts no one will open." Christ is therefore, in this instance, presented as the antitype of Eliakim. His key is to spiritual treasures—holiness and truth as mentioned in verse 7, as well as opportunity, service, and testimony as referred to in verse 8.

As with several of the other churches, He began with "I know your deeds," indicating His interest and familiarity with each church. In the case of Philadelphia, those words are followed by the comment that He had put before them an open door which no one could shut. This open door opportunity was protected because they had so little power and could not handle the challenge themselves; yet they had kept His word and not denied His name. He confirmed Paul's comment in 2 Corinthians 12:9, that His "grace is sufficient for you, for power is perfected in weakness." Just as He is today, Christ is the God of the open door and only when He provides the open door will there be substantial production of spiritual fruit. He appeared to be satisfied with this little church, in fact so much so He was going to trust them with an open door

Verses 9-11

The open door is an opportunity for effective service or to present the gospel (see 1 Corinthians 16:8-9; 2 Corinthians 2:12; Colossians 4:3), but there were adversaries. In this case it was again the synagogue of Satan, consisting of unbelieving Jews whom Christ did not recognize as Jews because they opposed the witness of the gospel here as they did in Smyrna. He promised this church victory over these adversaries and would cause the adversaries to bow down at the feet of the Philadelphians; these rebellious Jews would know that Christ loved this church. This open door opportunity was the reason many think of the Philadelphian church as a missionary church.

An outstanding promise was given to the church: He would keep them from the hour of testing which was about to come upon the whole world to test those who dwell upon the earth. This "hour of testing" appears to refer to the tribulation period, since the testing will affect the whole world and not just a local church. Further, the deliverance is from the "hour" (or time) of testing and not just from the test itself. Post-tribulationists have resisted this conclusion as unwarranted, but if this promise has any bearing on the rapture, it emphasizes deliverance *from* rather than *through* the hour of testing. This passage seems to provide further support for the hope that Christ will come for His Church before the time of trial and trouble described in Revelation chapters 6–19, and is further emphasized by His following comment that "I am coming quickly" ("quickly" in this context does not mean "soon," but "unexpectedly").

Verses 12-13

To Thyatira, Christ promised blessings that would occur at His second coming; similarly to Philadelphia, He promised blessings that would only occur at the time the new heaven and the new earth are introduced, indicating that both churches will be participants in His kingdom. To him who overcomes, He promised: (1) to make him a pillar in God's temple (a leader in the new Jerusalem); (2) that he would not go out from it anymore (not be exposed to temptation anymore); (3) to write upon him the name of His God, the name of the city of His God, (the new Jerusalem, which comes down out of heaven), and His new name.

Philadelphia is the only church for which Christ had no admonishment. The church of Philadelphia presents a wonderful model for churches of today. This is a church that, even though weak, kept His word and responded to the open doors that He provided. This church took advantage of opportunities to perform those deeds that He intended for them to perform as He paved the way and removed obstacles that would hinder their work.

CHURCH AT LAODICEA

The city of Laodicea was founded by Antiochus II in the third century B.C. and was named in honor of his wife Laodice. It was about forty miles southeast of Philadelphia. Under Roman rule it became wealthy from the production of wool cloth, and it was also a well known banking and money-changing center. Its medical school developed an eye salve from phrygia powder that was used extensively for the treatment of eye diseases. Destroyed by an earthquake about 60 A.D., it refused outside help and financed its own rebuilding.

Paul had not visited the church but apparently knew of it or knew of some of the Christians there as he mentioned them in his letter to the Colossians. Written about thirty years before John wrote Revelation, Paul's letter comments on how great a struggle he was having on behalf of the Christians at Colossae and Laodicea (Colossians 2:1). In Colossians 4:15, Paul instructed the Colossians to greet the brethren in Laodicea and to make sure the church at Laodicea also read the letter to the Colossians. He had also written a separate letter to the church at Laodicea, as mentioned in 4:16, so it must have been a church of some importance to Paul. It also appears that Paul had some misgivings about the church at Laodicea and its leadership, for in 4:17 he told the Colossians to pass on a message to Archippus, who was head of the church at Laodicea, "Take heed to the ministry which you have received in the Lord, that you may fulfill it." Possibly Archippus was the cause of Christ's concern thirty years later when He addressed this church in Revelation 3:14-22.

Verse 14

Christ addressed this church in an unusual way, calling Himself the Amen, meaning "so be it," quite often translated "verily" or "truly" or used as an ending to a prayer. When used by Christ, it is meant to be the final word and confirms Christ's absolute position as being the way and the truth (John 14:6). He followed this by further confirmation of

His position as "the faithful and true Witness," indicating that what He said about this church was a true analysis of its condition. His next statement, calling Himself "the Beginning of the creation of God" has caused some confusion among theologians over the years. Some believe this implies that He was created, but it does not imply that at all; instead, it means that He is the Creator and in Him the whole creation of God was begun. He is the source and primary fountainhead of all creation. Paul made this clear in Colossians 1:15-17, and the Laodiceans were quite aware of this as they had received and read that letter.

Verses 15-16

For all their familiarity with the writings of Paul, both to the Colossians and his letter to them (which has not been preserved), the Laodiceans apparently were not believers, for Christ gave them a scathing rebuke in verses 15 and 16, "I know your deeds, that you are neither cold nor hot; I would that you were cold or hot. So because you are lukewarm, and neither hot nor cold, I will spit you out of My mouth." Here we find a church that was neither cold (the normal spiritual condition before coming to Christ) nor hot (the transformed condition when a person becomes a believer, is filled with the Holy Spirit, and becomes interested in the things of God). They had been touched by the gospel, but it is not clear that they really belonged to Christ. It is remarkable that there are no words of commendation, but neither are there citations of departure in doctrine or morals as in the letters to the other churches. This would seem to indicate that all of the members of this church were lukewarm.

Verse 17

The church was a conceited church. It lacked spiritual perception, devotion, or faith. According to Christ, it was wealthy and felt it had need of nothing. It had obviously replaced its spiritual need by exalting riches and material goods. Their economic well being had blinded them to their spiritual need. In Christ's eyes, they were wretched, miserable, poor, blind, and naked. They had been lulled into false contentment by their material wealth—just the opposite of those at Smyrna who thought they were poor but were rich in Christ.

Verses 18-19

Christ addressed a word of counsel or advice to this church. He could command, but with a touch of irony He offered advice that they needed what they could not buy—gold (true riches), white garments (righteousness), and eye salve (discernment)—and that could only be obtained from Him. His message was a parody of those things that they already thought they had in abundance. He then called them to repent, for whom He loves He reproves and disciplines, an apparent reflection of the principle expounded by Paul in 1 Corinthians 11:31-32, wherein he explained that if we don't want to be judged, then we should judge ourselves rightly, otherwise the Lord will judge us and we will be disciplined.

Verse 20

This verse includes that famous passage, " I stand at the door and knock," rendered so effectively in a painting by William Hunt in 1854. That painting hangs in St. Paul's Cathedral in London where I have seen it several times. Christ is standing with a lantern in hand outside a cottage door. The door has no doorknob on the outside, representing that the door can only be opened from the inside. In Hunt's view, Christ will not force His way into the human heart; rather, He waits to be invited. Therefore, the door must be opened from the inside. This passage is frequently misused to represent Christ appealing to the sinner, requesting that he open the door to his heart in repentance so that Christ may come in and provide salvation. The true meaning, however, is Christ's offer of fellowship ("dine with him"), which He can only have with one who is a true disciple. The offer of fellowship is addressed to the church and to all who hear His voice who may have lost their way, who need to repent and renew their fellowship with Him. He is ready and willing to do just that if they will open the door and allow Him to fellowship with them.

Verses 21-22

The only cure for lukewarmness is a readmission of the excluded Christ. What a blessed condescension is revealed here in the attitude of

Christ. The creator awaits the decision of His creature, who is unworthy of any divine blessing, to accept His promise of renewed fellowship. If he overcomes as Christ did, Christ grants him permission to sit with Him on His throne. (Note: We know nothing of Christ's throne and only a bit about God's throne. The only throne we are fully aware of is David's throne, a worldly throne that Christ will occupy.) So, he who was about to be spewed out of the mouth of God for being lukewarm can share Christ's glory by repenting and opening the door to renew the precious fellowship.

This "lukewarmness" indicates a mixture of religiosity and the world. Some believe that the Laodicean church is representative of many churches today—a mixture of religion and worldliness. Apparently there is something about the intermediate state of being lukewarm that is utterly obnoxious to Christ. There are few passages in Scripture more searching, more condemning, more pointed than this message to the "church of the last days," as the Laodicean church has been called. I wonder if many of our churches of today may not be living the "Laodicean lie."

SUMMARY OF THE MESSAGES TO THE CHURCHES

This brings to a close the portion of Revelation described as "the things which are" in 1:19. As stated earlier, it seems that these letters represent Christ's personal comments to His bride, the church, and are those things which He considers of major concern as to her development during the "church age."

Though their deeds of perseverance, distaste of evil, testing false apostles, and not growing weary were commendable, Christ was concerned with the church at *Ephesus* losing its first love, or that love that is characteristic of those who believe in Him.

At *Smyrna*, though they were rich in faith, He was concerned that their fear of persecution might cause them to lose that faith.

The problem at *Pergamum* was doctrinal compromise. Even though they had endured persecution and the death of one of their group without losing faith or denying Christ's name, they were still in danger.

Thyatira's problem was moral compromise caused by a lack of understanding sound doctrine and the deep things of God, even though their love, faith, service, and perseverance were commendable and their deeds were even greater than at first.

Sardis was spiritually dead even though they put on a show and had a reputation of being alive. They had no commendable deeds. Their only hope was to wake up and repent.

Philadelphia was weak but had kept the word and not denied the Lord. Christ promised them His strength and an open door, as well as keeping them from the hour of testing that was to come upon the world.

Laodicea displayed an outer religiosity but had no zeal for the Lord. The church was lukewarm and Christ expressed His disdain for such a condition by saying He would spit them out of His mouth. They had no commendable virtues. Many consider Laodicea to be representative of the church in the last days.

THE RAPTURE AND THE TRIBULATION

The letters to the seven churches are now followed by judgments disclosed through the opening of seven seals, the blowing of seven trumpets, and the pouring out of seven bowls as we proceed through chapters 4 through 18. The church is mentioned nineteen times in the first three chapters, but is not mentioned again in chapters 4 through 18. Many believe, as do I, that the reason for this is the rapture, the term for Christ returning for His church and taking the believers with Him. (This is not the established church, but the body of true believers scattered throughout the established church.) The church may not be mentioned in these chapters because believers are not on earth during the tribulation period, which is covered in chapters 4 through 18.

A further thought regarding this conclusion is that the church is referred to as the "body of Christ." In 1 Corinthians 12:27 and again in Ephesians 5:22-30, Paul compared the relationship between wives and husbands to Christ and the church. "No one ever hated his own flesh, but nourishes and cherishes it, just as Christ also does the church, because we are members of His body" (Ephesians 5:29-30). In Paul's conversion on the road to Damascus, Christ asked him, "Why are you persecuting Me?" But Saul did not know Jesus, for he responded, "Who art Thou, Lord?" (Acts 9:4-5). Saul thought he was persecuting heretics, but in persecuting the church—the believers—he was persecuting Christ Himself. Through this disclosure in the interchange between Christ and Paul, we know that Jesus feels personally the persecution of His body, the church. Logic, as well as Scripture, leads us to assume that He will not put His body through the pain of the judgments that He will pour out on the earth.

The rapture is not mentioned in Revelation; the word "tribulation" is used only once in 7:14, but it is described in some detail in chapters 6 through 18. They are, however, closely related in eschatology. In order to enhance our study and understanding of Revelation, it is necessary to consider both of these subjects. It appears that the most appropriate place to do that is where we are now, between chapters 3 and 4. Consequently, we will insert a brief study of those subjects in here with the caveat, as mentioned above, that the term "rapture" is not used nor is it described in Revelation; however, it may be alluded to in the promise to keep the church at Philadelphia from the "hour of testing" (3:10).

The Tribulation

Since "rapture" is the term used to describe the escape of the church from the tribulation, we will first examine the scriptural evidence for the tribulation and the reasons we believe that the book of Revelation describes that terrible time upon the earth. To do so, however, we must begin with the Old Testament book of Daniel. The prophet Daniel gave a prophecy about seventy weeks, and it is in that great prophecy that we find the key to the chronology of end time events and their purpose. Daniel had been studying the writings of an earlier prophet, Jeremiah, and observed that the judgment against Jerusalem would last seventy years. In his deep distress, Daniel sought the Lord. He was in fervent prayer over the sins of Israel, asking the Lord's forgiveness, when the angel Gabriel came to give him "insight with understanding" (Daniel 9:22). Gabriel proceeded to give Daniel the message recorded in Daniel 9:24-27, a passage of Scripture that has been called "the backbone of prophecy."

In summary, that message informed Daniel that seventy weeks had been decreed for his people (Israel) to accomplish six objectives: (1) to finish the transgression, (2) to make an end of sin, (3) to make atonement for iniquity, (4) to bring in everlasting righteousness, (5) to seal up vision and prophecy, and (6) to anoint the most holy place. Gabriel continued his message, telling Daniel that from the issuing of a decree to restore and rebuild Jerusalem until the Messiah, the Prince, there would be sixty-nine weeks (actually in two parts: seven weeks plus sixty-two weeks) after which "the Messiah will be cut off and have nothing, and the people of the prince who is to come will destroy the city and the sanctuary." Then "he [the prince who is to come] will make a firm covenant with the many [Israel] for one week, but in the middle of the week he will put a stop to sacrifice and grain offering; and on the wing of abominations will come one who makes desolate" until he is destroyed as decreed. Nearly all commentators agree that the "weeks" refer to years, so that this prophecy covers a period of seventy "weeks" of years, or 490 years. There are several reasons for this conclusion, but these will not be covered at this point.

Within this prophecy are several points to be considered:

(1) The seventy weeks of years (490 years) were decreed for Daniel's people, or Israel; consequently the 490 years are a timeline related to Israel and only consequentially to the rest of the world.

(2) There were six specific purposes to be accomplished during this time (noted above). Although some commentators believe that all six of these have already been fulfilled, others believe that possibly some were fulfilled by Christ's first advent but they will not all be fulfilled until His second coming. Still others believe that all six of these purposes will all be fulfilled at Christ's second coming.

(3) There will be sixty-nine "weeks" between issuing the decree to rebuild Jerusalem and when the Messiah will be cut off. There have been four different decrees from different dates recorded in 2 Chronicles, Ezra, and Nehemiah regarding the rebuilding of either Jerusalem or the temple. There is disagreement among commentators as to which decree is appropriate to use. However, since the city is mentioned in the prophecy and the decree to rebuild the city was not issued until Nehemiah's time, I would work from the decree recorded in Nehemiah 2:8 in his twentieth

year (444 B.C.) when Artaxerxes gave Nehemiah authorization to go to Judah to rebuild Jerusalem. Using that date and projecting forward 483 years (69 x 7) the result is A.D. 33, the year it is thought that Christ was crucified ("cut off").

(4) After the Messiah is cut off, the people of "the prince who is to come" will destroy the city and the sanctuary. Rome destroyed Jerusalem and the temple in 70 A.D., thirty-seven years after Christ's crucifixion. Since "the prince who is to come" is thought to be the antichrist, this raises the question of whether he will be a Roman or from the Roman Empire. Since the prophecy concerns only Israel, I believe the reference could be generic and refer to Gentiles in general. As we will see later, however, there is good reason to believe he will be of Middle-Eastern origin.

(5) He ("the prince who is to come") will make a covenant with the "many" (Israel) for one week, but in the middle of the week will put a stop to sacrifices and "on the wing of abominations will come one who makes desolate" until he is destroyed. This refers to the last week of the prophecy of the seventy weeks of years, or the last seven years of the 490 years. Most commentators agree that this refers to the time of the antichrist.

There is, then, a break between the sixty-ninth week (483rd year) and the seventieth week, known as the church age (the age in which we live). The antichrist apparently will have the position and authority to enter into a seven-year covenant with Israel at the beginning of that seventieth week. That covenant apparently has to do with the temple, for he abrogates the agreement at the end of three-and-a-half years by stopping the people from giving sacrifices and grain offerings.

Then comes one on the "wing of abominations," meaning that he desecrates the temple as did Antiochus Epiphanes in Daniel 11:31. The temple does not now exist; it must be built, probably as part of the covenant. The phrase "on the wing of abominations will come one" seems to refer to a second person; if so, it is undoubtedly the false prophet who arises to assist the antichrist (we will discuss the false prophet further in chapter 13). I believe, however, that this probably refers to the change that comes over the antichrist at the midpoint, or the three-and-a-half year point of his reign, for at that time he will become like a different person after his apparent death. This will be discussed in some detail later.

Most commentators believe that this last period of seven years during which the prince to come, or antichrist, dominates the world, is the tribulation period; the last three-and-a-half years of which is the great tribulation. Christ confirmed both Daniel's prophecy and the fact that it pertained to the end times and the tribulation period when He mentioned the "ABOMINATION OF DESOLATION which was spoken of through Daniel the prophet" as a sign of the end time and time of tribulation (see Matthew 24:15). There is much more to consider regarding the antichrist, but there will be opportunity to explore those matters as we proceed through Revelation.

Other scriptures speak of the tribulation as a time of judgment of Israel which will occur on the earth during the last days of human history. This time of judgment and distress is spoken of four times in Scripture where it is described as a unique, one-time event that has dramatic characteristics. It is first described as the "time of Jacob's distress" in Jeremiah 30:2-11 where the Lord says to Jeremiah,

> *"Days are coming," declares the LORD, "when I will restore the fortunes of My people Israel and Judah." The LORD says, "I will also bring them back to the land that I gave to their forefathers, and they shall possess it."... "Alas! for that day is great, there is none like it; and it is the time of Jacob's distress, but he will be saved from it...For I am with you," declares the LORD, "to save you; for I will destroy completely all the nations where I have scattered you, only I will not destroy you completely. But I will chasten you justly, and will by no means leave you unpunished."*
> —Jeremiah 30:3, 7, 11

In Daniel 12:1 much the same message appears:

> *Now at that time Michael, the great prince who stands guard over the sons of your people, will arise. And there will be a time of distress such as never occurred since there was a nation until that time; and at that time your people, everyone who is found written in the book, will be rescued.*

Joel 2:1-2 express it more dramatically as "the day of the LORD":

Blow a trumpet in Zion, and sound an alarm on My holy mountain! Let all the inhabitants of the land tremble, for the day of the LORD is coming; surely it is near, a day of darkness and gloom, a day of clouds and thick darkness. As the dawn is spread over the mountains, so there is a great and mighty people; there has never been anything like it, nor will there be again after it to the years of many generations.

The time is then confirmed and called the "great tribulation" by Jesus in Matthew 24:15-16 and 21-22. In verses 15-16, Jesus states,

Therefore when you see the ABOMINATION OF DESOLATION which was spoken of through Daniel the prophet, standing in the holy place (let the reader understand), then let those who are in Judea flee to the mountains.

In verses 21-22 He continues,

For then there will be a great tribulation, such as has not occurred since the beginning of the world until now, nor ever shall. And unless those days had been cut short, no life would have been saved; but for the sake of the elect those days shall be cut short.

It should be noted that the "elect" referred to by Jesus is considered by some to be the church, but the church will have already been raptured. Others believe it refers to those redeemed during the church age, and this is a possibility. I believe, however, that when considered in the context of the Old Testament scriptures set forth above, the "elect" refers to Israel. In each Scripture passage is a promise that a remnant will be saved, and each of the authors at that time were talking to and about Israel.

The tribulation is further spoken of in several passages in the minor prophets. Its unique characteristic is not mentioned, although it is frequently spoken of as "the day of the LORD" (as in Joel 2:1-2). The uniqueness of that time is certainly implied by the fearful phenomenon of events that are described—events that have not yet occurred on the earth. In Joel 2:30-31 is written:

And I will display wonders in the sky and on the earth, blood, fire, and columns of smoke. The sun will be turned into darkness, and the moon into blood, before the great and awesome day of the LORD comes.

Amos 5:18 says:

Alas, you who are longing for the day of the LORD, for what purpose will the day of the LORD be to you? It will be darkness and not light.

Zephaniah sets forth a terrible time. In 1:14-15 he states,

Near is the great day of the LORD, near and coming quickly; listen, the day of the LORD! In it the warrior cries bitterly. A day of wrath is that day, a day of trouble and distress, a day of destruction and desolation, a day of darkness and gloom, a day of clouds and thick darkness.

Zephaniah closes his description in 1:18,

And all the earth will be devoured in the fire of His jealousy, for He will make a complete end, indeed a terrifying one, of all the inhabitants of the earth.

As noted above, the prophecy in Daniel 9:27 refers to the covenant that the "prince who is to come" enters into with Israel, a covenant that he then breaks in the middle of the week or at the end of three-and-a-half years. This time period of three-and-one-half years is mentioned several times in Scripture in various ways. In Daniel 7:25 and 12:7, and in Revelation 12:14, this time period is referred to as "time, times, and half a time." In Revelation 11:3 and 12:6 it is referred to as 1,260 days. In Daniel 12:11, it is referred to as 1,290 days. There is no explanation of why the extra thirty days are added in Daniel, although there are logical speculations as to the reason. In Revelation 11:2 and 13:5, the time period is referred to as forty-two months. We will consider each of these Scriptures as we proceed through Revelation, but suffice it to say at this point that they all seem to refer to the same period of time, the last three-and-a-half years of the tribulation, otherwise known as the "great tribulation" (7:14). They are presented here to indicate the

consistency of references in Scripture to this time period and to indicate the relationship between the various scriptures. With each of these
time references there is a description of different events, so when put
together they give us an idea as to what events take place during these
three-and-a-half years.

The purpose of the tribulation is further spoken of in Malachi 4:1-4,
where the Lord describes the coming day that will burn the arrogant and
evildoer (see also Revelation 16:8). In verses 5-6, the Lord says to Israel,
"Behold, I am going to send you Elijah the prophet before the coming
of the great and terrible day of the LORD And he will restore the hearts
of the fathers to their children, and the hearts of the children to their
fathers, lest I come and smite the land with a curse." Elijah may very
well be one of the two witnesses who appears on the scene and whom
we will consider in Revelation 11.

The Rapture

There are several positions taken by Bible students regarding the
rapture, and as might be expected, it is a subject about which Bible
students have the most disagreement. In general, these various positions
are described as amillennial, postmillennial, and premillennial. Each of
these positions consider the thousand-year reign of Christ, disclosed in
Revelation 20, from a different perspective. Although the millennium
is not part of our consideration at this point, those who hold these
various views of that event also hold differing views of the tribulation
and the rapture.

Briefly, *amillennialists* believe that there will be no tribulation,
rapture, or millennial kingdom. They believe that scriptural passages
regarding the millennium are being fulfilled on earth at the present
time during the church age or are being fulfilled by saints in heaven
now. They consider that God's covenants with Israel are fulfilled by the
church spiritually and that the new heaven and earth immediately follow the church age and consummate history. They employ non-literal
and spiritual interpretive principles regarding eschatology, but normal
literal interpretation in all other areas. Their scriptural support is basically
Ephesians 3:4-5, where Paul claimed the mystery of Christ was "not made
known" in other generations, which they interpret as indicating that the

church was actually in the Old Testament even though undisclosed. They believe that the promise of land to Israel was fulfilled during the time of Joshua (Joshua 21:43-45) or under Solomon (1 Kings 4:21). They believe that the seventy weeks mentioned in Daniel's prophecy are of an imprecise duration and refer to the entire church age. They are also of the opinion that Satan has been bound, as prophesied in Revelation 20:2, throughout the church age. The great leaders of the Reformation were amillennialists. Martin Luther believed he was in the great tribulation, and Calvin taught that Israel and the church were the same in Scripture. This thought is currently popular in that it emphasizes the spiritual church rather than Israel's earthly kingdom. It does, however, seem to ignore Paul's warning in Romans 11:18-27 that Gentiles should be neither arrogant nor ignorant regarding the ultimate restoration of Israel at the time the fullness of the Gentiles has come in.

Postmillennialism holds that the kingdom of God is being extended in the world through preaching the gospel and the work of the Holy Spirit. The world will eventually be Christianized and Christ will return after a long period of righteousness on earth called the millennium. The scriptural support for this position is extensive as they interpret those Scriptures regarding the kingdom age to be applicable to this age as many nations come to worship the Lord in Jerusalem (Scriptures such as Psalms 68; 72; 102; Isaiah 2; 11:6-9; Jeremiah 31:34). This belief precludes, of course, both the tribulation and the rapture. Postmillennialism is no longer popular and has declined in acceptance.

Premillennialists interpret biblical prophecies just as they do other portions of Scripture, that is, in a literal sense. They hold that the second coming of Christ will be followed by His reign for a thousand years as disclosed in Revelation 20. They also believe in the tribulation and that it will occur just before the millennium. They believe there will be a rapture but are in disagreement as to its timing in relation to the tribulation and who will be included; consequently, premillennialists have been divided according to the most distinguishing features of their respective beliefs—pretribulationists (pretrib), midtribulationists (midtrib), posttribulationists (posttrib), and partial rapturists.

As these titles would imply, the *pretribs* believe the rapture will occur before the tribulation begins. This position is discussed below in detail.

Midtribs believe the church will go through the first three-and-a-half years, since that period will be dominated by the antichrist and the church is not promised relief from his persecution. The church will, however, be delivered before the wrath of God falls upon the earth during the last three-and-a-half years or the great tribulation. To hold this position, midtribs deny the doctrine of the imminent return of Christ for His church (the rapture) and the strict distinction between Israel and the church.

Posttribs believe that the church will go through the entire tribulation period of seven years. They do not believe the church is promised relief from any of the tribulation, but that it will be caught up, as per 1 Thessalonians 4, as Christ is descending from heaven at His second coming and will then continue with Him to earth. Their belief is based upon Matthew 28:20 where Christ says, "I am with you always, even to the end of the age"; and Matthew 24:9-11 as Christ says, "Then they will deliver you to tribulation, and will kill you, and you will be hated by all nations on account of My name." Jesus' words were addressed to Israel, not the church, but posttribs deny the distinction between Israel and the church.

Partial rapturists believe that the rapture will occur before the tribulation, as do the pretribs, but only those who are looking for Christ will be delivered at that time whereas the rest of the church will have to endure the tribulation period. This is based primarily on Hebrews 9:28, "So Christ also, having been offered once to bear the sins of many, shall appear a second time for salvation without reference to sin, to those who eagerly await Him."

The primary Scripture upon which the pretribs base their belief in a rapture, and to which I concur, is 1 Thessalonians 4:13-18. Paul was concerned about the Thessalonians' belief that they had to be alive when Christ returned; otherwise, they would miss out on that day and would have no hope. He, therefore, instructed them:

> *We do not want you to be uninformed, brethren, about those who are asleep, that you may not grieve, as do the rest who have no hope. For if we believe that Jesus died and rose again, even so God will bring with Him those who have fallen asleep in Jesus. For this we say to you by the word of the Lord, that we who are alive, and remain until the coming*

of the Lord, shall not precede those who have fallen asleep. For the Lord Himself will descend from heaven with a shout, with the voice of the archangel, and with the trumpet of God; and the dead in Christ shall rise first. Then we who are alive and remain shall be caught up together with them in the clouds to meet the Lord in the air, and thus we shall always be with the Lord.

—1 Thessalonians 4:13-18

We also have that great promise in John 14:1-3 where Christ reassures His disciples; "Let not your heart be troubled; believe in God, believe also in Me. In My Father's house are many dwelling places; if it were not so, I would have told you; for I go to prepare a place for you. And if I go and prepare a place for you, I will come again, and receive you to Myself, that where I am there you may be also." Other verses implying that there will be a rapture are 1 Corinthians 15:51-52 where Paul states, "Behold, I tell you a mystery; we shall not all sleep, but we shall all be changed, in a moment, in the twinkling of an eye, at the last trumpet; for the trumpet will sound, and the dead will be raised imperishable, and we shall be changed." This statement is very close to the one in 1 Thessalonians 4 (quoted above) indicating that both the living and the dead will be included in the event announced by a trumpet. Then in 2 Thessalonians 2:1 Paul tells those in Thessalonica, "With regard to the coming of our Lord Jesus Christ, and our gathering together with Him..." Note that he referred to our "gathering together" with Christ, which seems to refer to his earlier message in 1 Thessalonians 4 and our meeting the Lord in the air.

In addition to those Scriptures that contain a positive message of how we will be delivered by the intervention of the Lord, there are several that indicate that those who believe in Christ will not be subject to the trials of the tribulation. There would seem to be only one way to avoid this judgment which is to come upon the whole world, and that is removal from the earth prior to the time of trial. In 1 Thessalonians 1:10 we are told to "wait for His Son from heaven, whom He raised from the dead, that is Jesus, who delivers us from the wrath to come." In 1 Thessalonians 5:9, Paul wrote, "For God has not destined us for wrath, but for obtaining salvation through our Lord Jesus Christ." Romans 5:8-9 states, "But God demonstrates His own love toward us, in that while we were yet sinners, Christ died for us. Much more then, having now been justified by His blood, we shall be saved from the wrath of God through Him." All three of these Scriptures refer to believers' salvation or deliverance from the wrath to come through Christ who suffered the wrath of His Father for us when He died on the cross. Since He suffered for us, it only makes sense that we would not have to also suffer God's wrath as will the rest of the world.

In Revelation 3:10 we read His promise to the church at Philadelphia," Because you have kept the word of My perseverance, I also will keep you from the hour of testing, that hour which is about to come upon the whole world, to test those who dwell upon the earth." The wrath spoken of in these verses is that same wrath spoken of by John the Baptist to the Sadducees and Pharisees in Matthew 3:7, "You brood of vipers, who warned you to flee from the wrath to come?" and by Paul in Romans 3:5-6, "The God who inflicts wrath is not unrighteous, is He?...May it never be! For otherwise how will God judge the world?" And again, in Revelation 6:16-17, "They said to the mountains and to the rocks, 'Fall on us and hide us from the presence of Him who sits on the throne, and from the wrath of the Lamb; for the great day of their wrath has come, and who is able to stand?'" The "wrath of God" is referred to throughout Revelation (11:18; 14:10, 19; 15:1, 7 ; 16:1; 19:15) leaving no doubt as to the cause and purpose of the events described in that book nor the wrath from which the church will be delivered.

The Rapture and the Second Coming

A major consideration that leads me to believe that there will be a rapture in addition to the second coming is the distinctive difference between the two events. In Matthew 24:29-30, Christ told His disciples that immediately after the tribulation of those days, "the tribes of the earth will mourn, and will see the SON OF MAN COMING ON THE CLOUDS OF THE SKY with power and great glory." This same message is repeated in Mark 13:26 and Luke 21:27. And then comes that great description in Revelation 19:11-16,

> *And I saw heaven opened; and behold, a white horse, and He who sat upon it is called Faithful and True; and in righteousness He judges and*

wages war. And His eyes are a flame of fire, and upon His head are many diadems; and He has a name written upon Him which no one knows except Himself. And He is clothed with a robe dipped in blood; and His name is called, The Word of God. And the armies which are in heaven, clothed in fine linen, white and clean, were following Him on white horses. And from His mouth comes a sharp sword, so that with it He may smite the nations; and He will rule them with a rod of iron; and He treads the wine press of the fierce wrath of God, the Almighty. And on His robe and on His thigh He has a name written, "KING OF KINGS, AND LORD OF LORDS."

This powerful description of the Lord's second coming is quite a different picture than the one portrayed in 1 Thessalonians 4 regarding the rapture.

One other major difference is that the second coming will be preceded by signs indicating that it is coming soon; there are no signs preceding the rapture, however. This is emphasized by Christ in His Olivet discourse in Matthew 24 where He answered the disciples' question; "Tell us, when will these things be, and what will be the sign of Your coming, and of the end of the age?" (Matthew 24:3). He proceeded to give them an outline of things which would occur on earth just prior to His coming and concluded in verses 32-34, "Now learn the parable from the fig tree: when its branch has already become tender, and puts forth its leaves, you know summer is near; even so you too, when you see all these things, recognize that He is near, right at the door. Truly I say to you, this generation will not pass away until all these things take place."

In contrast to these specifics regarding the second coming, there are no preceding signs mentioned relative to the rapture (doctrine of imminence). There are, however, several admonitions to be alert, watch, and be ready. In fact, the early believers thought He was coming back within their lifetimes; thus, Paul had to write the Thessalonians and assure them they had not missed the day of the Lord (2 Thessalonians 2:1-3). Some of these Scriptures that may have led them to believe in the imminent return were: "I will come again, and receive you to Myself" (John 14:3), "In a moment, in the twinkling of an eye, at the last trumpet; for the trumpet will sound, and the dead will be raised imperishable, and we shall be changed" (1 Corinthians 15:52), "You too be patient; strengthen your hearts, for the coming of the Lord is at hand"(James 5:8), "For our citizenship is in heaven, from which also we eagerly wait for a Savior, the Lord Jesus Christ" (Philippians 3:20), "Looking for the blessed hope and the appearing of the glory of our great God and Savior, Christ Jesus" (Titus 2:13).

Then, there is one other important comment by Jesus in Matthew 23:37-39 that sets the second coming apart from the rapture, which seems to have been ignored by most commentators as a prophetic statement. As He looked out over Jerusalem and was agonizing over her disobedience, He said, "How often I wanted to gather your children together, the way a hen gathers her chicks under her wings, and you were unwilling. Behold, your house is being left to you desolate! For I say to you, from now on you shall not see Me until you say, 'BLESSED IS HE WHO COMES IN THE NAME OF THE LORD.'" In this statement, Christ seems to be confirming the judgment against Israel from Isaiah 6:9-10 wherein God rendered their hearts insensitive, their ears dull, and their eyes dim lest they see, hear, understand, and return and be healed. As He looked out over Jerusalem, Christ was saying that the day will come they will call for Him, and He will return and heal them. This will occur at the end of the tribulation as Israel's eyes, ears, and hearts will be open and sensitive; they will recognize their mistake in rejecting their Messiah and they will come to Him. I believe that Elijah, who is thought to be one of the two witnesses mentioned in Revelation 11, will play a major part in this awakening, as prophesied in Malachi 4:5.

Another strong indicator that a rapture does occur is the marriage supper of the Lamb, which takes place in Revelation 19:7-9, just prior to Christ's return (described in 19:11). The marriage supper takes place before His second coming is described; therefore, the church would have to be in heaven prior to His return; for that to be the case, the believers would have to have been ushered there previously—in the rapture. There are other matters which imply that a rapture has occurred which I will comment upon as they arise.

We now return to Revelation and "the things which shall take place after these things" (1:19). In proceeding, it should be noted that my comments relative to the remainder of Revelation are based upon the belief that the rapture has occurred and that the subject of chapters 4 through 18 is the tribulation period. It should also be noted that the scriptural presentation will move between those thing happening on earth and those things happening in heaven; it will be important to keep in mind the location of the scenario being described. In general, those things in or from heaven cannot and will not be seen by those living on earth.

REVELATION 4

Verses 1-3

John was introduced to events in heaven by the voice he identified as the one he first heard in chapter 1—the voice of Christ. He saw a door standing open in heaven, and the voice, like the sound of a trumpet, instructed him to "come up here, and I will show you what must take place after these things." The open door reminds us of Christ's comment in John 10:9, "I am the door; if anyone enters through Me, he shall be saved." Only through Christ can salvation and entry to heaven be attained.

The first thing John saw in heaven was the manifestation of One on His throne in a montage of light and color. His appearance was like a jasper (clear white) stone and sardius (blood red); there was an emerald rainbow around the throne. John does not tell us who this was, probably because he did not know. He was told to write only what he saw; he was not instructed to investigate and explain his vision. Many believe that this was Jesus; however, I agree with others who believe it was more likely God hidden from view by His glory, a glory that would have destroyed John had he looked directly upon it.

The colors are significant to Israel who, it has been pointed out, is the main focus of Revelation. In Exodus 28:15-21, God instructed Israel to include certain stones mounted in rows on the breastpiece of judgment, a part of the holy garments for Aaron, the high priest. These stones were to be according to the names of the twelve tribes of Israel in the order of their birth. The first was ruby or sardius, representing Reuben, the firstborn of Jacob, and the last was jasper representing Benjamin, the last born of Jacob. It is interesting to note that here in Revelation the sequence is reversed: jasper is the first and sardius is the last. Whatever the reason, these stones represent the first and the last, just as Christ stated in 1:17. Jesus' words about being the first and the last and these specific stones would cause Israel to make the connection. The rainbow is familiar to Israel since the time of Noah when the Lord promised to never again destroy the world in judgment without a measure of mercy for a remnant (Genesis 9:12-17). Ezekiel saw a similar vision to John's in Ezekiel 1:28.

Verse 4

John next observed twenty-four thrones with twenty-four elders sitting on them clothed in white and wearing gold crowns. Again, he did not identify these people, and there have been many different inter-pretations of their identity—some say angels, some say representatives of the twelve tribes and the twelve apostles, some say representatives of the church which has been raptured. There are rather strong opinions among scholars that these are angels. It should be noticed, however, when we get to chapter 5, the elders are set out separately from angels, so whoever they are, it appears they are not angels.

There are several considerations which would lead us to the conclu-sion that these could be representatives of the church. The rapture has occurred; therefore, the church will be in heaven and could have repre-sentatives before God's throne. They are called "elders," which is a term most often used in connection with leaders of the church (1 Timothy 5:17). In both the Old and New Testaments, however, Israel also had elders as leaders in their government administration. The twenty-four elders are dressed in white garments (symbol of holiness); some believe that only the church will be so dressed, based upon Revelation 3:5. Some believe the crowns of gold are victors' crowns, which are only given to the church (1 Corinthians 9:25; James 1:12). The only time a gold crown is otherwise mentioned, however, is in 14:14 where it is worn by "one like a son of man" as He is ready to reap the harvest from the earth. So we have no clear indications of what these crowns may signify. From this verse we might consider them indicators of judgment and power or authority.

That the elders are a representative group seems probable as it would parallel the organization described for the priesthood in 1 Chronicles 24. David divided the levitical priests, who were many thousands, into twenty-four groups, so when the twenty-four elders met, one from each group, they represented thousands of priests. But there is no evidence that these twenty-four elders around the throne are either a representative group or, if so, whom they represent. Their identity, if they represent the church, would serve only as further indication that the rapture had taken place. That they represent the church is not clear, however, from the text.

I believe it is possible that this is a court of judgment. Daniel appears to have had a vision similar to John. In Daniel 7:9, he describes a court that is convened, "I kept looking until thrones were set up, and the Ancient of Days took His seat." Daniel does not indicate how many thrones were set up but proceeds to describe the Ancient of Days and His throne, closing verse 10 with the words, "The court sat, and the books were opened." From the verses that precede and follow verses 9 and 10, we can conclude that this court was convened to judge the "beast" or antichrist. This is further confirmed in verses 16-27, where Daniel asked for the exact meaning of the vision. In verse 26, Daniel stated that "the court will sit for judgment, and his [the beast or kingdom] dominion will be taken away, annihilated and destroyed forever." There is no indication by John that what he saw and described in Revelation was a court, but the similarities between what he saw and what Daniel observed lead me to that conclusion.

Also, the timing of John's vision, just before the judgments of Revelation begin, would indicate that it was a court of judgment. John comments in 20:4 that he saw "thrones, and they sat upon them, and judgment was given to them." God may have included the twenty-four elders in His court as observers or witnesses, or more likely they were participants in the dispensing of the judgments He was about to impose upon Israel and the world. The twelve apostles could certainly sit on twelve of the thrones. Christ told His disciples that when He sat on His glorious throne, "You also shall sit upon twelve thrones, judging the twelve tribes of Israel" (Matthew 19:28). We have no indication of who the other twelve of the twenty-four might be; however, Christ did say to the churches in 3:21 that he who overcomes will sit down with Him on His throne. He does not mention any participation in judgment, however.

Verses 5-8

John next described his view of the throne from which proceed lightning and thunder and before which there are seven lamps of fire, identified as the seven Spirits of God. The lightning and thunder are the manifestation of God as He appeared to Israel in the Old Testament, such as to Moses on Mount Sinai (Exodus 19:18-19). The seven lamps representing the seven Spirits of God were first mentioned by John in 1:4 as being before the throne. These represent the Holy Spirit, as described in Isaiah 11:2.

John described what looked like a sea of glass before the throne. In the center and around the throne were four living creatures full of eyes in front and behind, each of these creatures having different characteristics. The first creature was like a lion; the second creature was like a calf; the third creature had a face like that of a man; the fourth creature was like a flying eagle. They each have six wings, and day and night they continually praise God as holy, the one who was and who is and who is to come. There is no indication of what the sea of glass represents, however we do have an idea of who the four living creatures are based on visions of Ezekiel and Isaiah.

In Ezekiel 1:4-10, the prophet saw similar beings; however, they had human form and each had four faces—of a man, a lion, a bull, and an eagle—and four wings with human hands under the wings. Their facial features were similar to John's likenesses, but John implied that the whole being was as he had described, for he noted each of the creatures was like the characteristics described (except the third which had the face of a man). In chapter 10, Ezekiel saw these beings again and indicated that they were the same ones he had seen before. This time, however, he described their faces the same as before except the face of a bull became the face of a cherub, and he called the beings "cherubim" (Ezekiel 10:2).

Isaiah also saw similar beings, which he described in Isaiah 6. He had a vision of heaven and the Lord sitting on His throne. He saw standing above the throne beings with six wings chanting a praise to the Lord very similar to John's vision. He did not indicate how many there were, but did indicate they had only one face—about which he makes no remark so apparently it was not of unusual characteristic—and he called them "seraphim" (Isaiah 6:2).

From these descriptions we can conclude that they were angels, those having four wings being cherubim and those with six wings being seraphim. We can also conclude that the beings that John saw were angels, either cherubim or seraphim that were apparently especially sensitive to God's attributes for their primary function was to accompany and continually (day and night) bring honor, glory, and thanks to Him. They also have certain responsibilities both in worship, as we have seen, and in the execution of the judgments to come, as we will see. They may also have some relationship to the created world as evidenced by their characteristics as familiar created beings, their involvement in judgments to come over God's creation, and the focus on creation in the elders' response to the four beings in verse 11.

Verses 9-11

These verses describe an unusual scene, a repetitious reaction between the four beings and the twenty-four elders. As the four beings continually say, "HOLY, HOLY, HOLY, IS THE LORD GOD, THE ALMIGHTY, who was and who is and who is to come," the twenty-four elders fall down before God, worship Him, and cast their crowns before the throne, saying, "Worthy art Thou, our Lord and our God, to receive glory and honor and power; for Thou didst create all things, and because of Thy will they existed, and were created." Such a scene sounds like a repetitious rote and raises questions as to how the crowns are returned to the elders for the next round. I do not understand the significance of the repetition, but it does appear to be a worshipful, continual glorification of our great God and an exercise in which the elders cast their personal treasures before the One who bestowed them.

REVELATION 5

Verse 1

John continued his view of heaven begun in chapter 4 and the focus of his attention turned to the right hand of Him whom he saw sitting on the throne. He saw a book written on both sides, which was probably in the form of a scroll that was sealed with seven seals. The nature of the book has been the subject of some speculation by scholars.

Some think it was the book of life mentioned several times in Scripture from Exodus 32:32 to Revelation 21:27. Others believe it was a title deed to the earth, similar to the deed of purchase for land given to Jeremiah in Jeremiah 32, with the covenants of ownership being the judgments to be inflicted upon the earth. However, this latter conclusion seems to be in conflict with Daniel 7:13 where, following the court scene mentioned earlier, Christ came up to the Ancient of Days and was given dominion, glory, and a kingdom. This is after the "beast was slain" according to Daniel 7:11, so apparently, if there is to be any title deeds given to Christ, it will be after the antichrist is dispensed with. However, there are no documents mentioned nor, I suspect, needed for God to give Christ dominion, glory, and a kingdom.

The book that John saw in God's right hand was probably the one mentioned in Daniel 10 through 12. In Daniel 10:14, one who appeared to Daniel in a vision (it was most likely Gabriel, since he was mentioned as the messenger in Daniel 8:16 in a previous vision) says, "Now I have come to give you an understanding of what will happen to your people in the latter days, for the vision pertains to the days yet future." He continued in verse 21, "However, I will tell you what is inscribed in the writing of truth," or some translations use Book of Truth. The angel then proceeded to inform Daniel of the rise and fall of various powers in chapter 11 and concluded with the reign of the antichrist in 11:36-45. He continued in chapter 12 with a mention of the tribulation and the resurrection of both the righteous and the wicked (the only time this is mentioned in the Old Testament). Then in 12:4, he told Daniel, "But as for you, Daniel, conceal these words and seal up the book until the end of time; many will go back and forth, and knowledge will increase."

After this instruction, the angel and two of his companions discussed among themselves the message being sealed up, which we will refer to later, and the angel repeated his instruction to Daniel in 12:9 saying, "Go your way, Daniel, for these words are concealed and sealed up until the end time." From the information the angel revealed from the Book of Truth, the book appears to be a record of the Gentile rulers, past and future, of the nation of Israel. Both of these instructions to Daniel included the phrase, "until the end time," indicating that this book, the Book of Truth, will be opened at the end time. Referring back to 12:4, it is interesting to note that the angel tacked on the phrase, "many will go back and forth, and knowledge will increase," to define the "end time." That seems to define our present time very succinctly.

Verses 2-5

John next observed a strong angel proclaiming in a loud voice, looking for someone worthy to open the book. But no one in heaven, on earth, or under the earth was found worthy to open or look into the book. John was so disturbed that no one could be found to open or look into the book that he began to cry.

This is a rather interesting scene. Why was the angel calling out the need to find someone "worthy" and why was John so disturbed? Any answer to these questions would have to be speculation, but it reminds me of the familiar story of King Arthur and the sword Excalibur. If you recall, the sword had been lodged in a stone and only the one true king would be able to remove it. A search was instituted and anyone interested in trying to dislodge the sword had the opportunity, but none could remove it for none were qualified. So it was here. A search was evidently instituted in heaven, on the earth, and even in Hades (under the earth), but no one could be found who was worthy. John's emotional distress was probably due to his expectation that Christ would be the one to open the book, but when, after what must have been a thorough search, He did not appear, John was concerned. John's relationship with Christ had undoubtedly been close, for John called himself "the disciple whom Jesus loved" (John 13:23; 20:2; 21:7, 20) and he probably felt he understood Christ's message and position in the Father. In his Gospel, John quoted Jesus as He spoke to some doubting Jews regarding His relationship to the Father (John 5:19-27). Jesus said, "Not even the Father judges anyone, but He has given all judgment to the Son" (verse 22), and "He gave Him authority to execute judgment, because He is the Son of Man" (verse 27). John probably expected Christ to appear and immediately open the book; when He did not, John may have felt sorrow that he had somehow failed Jesus and misunderstood His message. Further, John had seen Christ in all His glory in the vision he recorded in chapter 1; this would have added to his expectation of Christ being the worthy one.

In order to relieve John's distress, one of the elders told John to stop weeping; the Lion from the tribe of Judah (representing the correct lineage of Christ—Genesis 49:8-10 and Matthew 1:1-3), the Root of David (the term "of" indicating He was both before and greater than David—2 Samuel 7:11-16; Isaiah 9:7; Matthew 22:41-45) had overcome and was able to open the book and the seven seals.

Verses 6-7

There then appeared a Lamb standing, as if slain, having seven horns and seven eyes, which are the seven Spirits of God. This is a picture of Christ, the humble, sacrificial Lamb of God (John 1:29, 36; 1 Peter 1:19), full of the Holy Spirit (represented by the seven spirits of God—Isaiah 11:1-2) in His resurrected body and in the fullness of His omnipotence, omniscience, and omnipresence. The Lamb was standing—evidence that He was alive. The phrase, "as if slain," seems to indicate that the marks of His torture and death are still fully visible on His body. He came and took the book out of the right hand of Him who sat on the throne, further evidence that the One on the throne was God, the Father. Christ, the Lamb who was slain, not the Christ of power and glory, is full of the Holy Spirit with wisdom, understanding, knowledge, and righteousness. He alone is worthy; He alone has the authority and sovereignty to execute the judgments called for in the book. He will judge, not by what His eyes see nor His ears hear, but with righteousness and fairness (Isaiah 11:3-4).

Verses 8-10

Crying ceased and worship began as the four living creatures and twenty-four elders fell down before the Lamb, each having a harp and a golden bowl full of incense which are the prayers of the saints (Psalm 141:2), symbolic of the importance in heaven of prayers coming from saints on earth. Then they sang a new song of redemption and declaration of Christ's being worthy to take the book and break the seals: "Worthy are You to take the book, and to break its seals; for You were slain, and purchased for God with Your blood men from every tribe and tongue and people and nation. You have made them to be a kingdom and priests to our God; and they will reign upon the earth."

Verses 11-14

As thousands upon thousands of angels join in the praise, a distinction is made between angels, the living creatures, and the elders—from which we can conclude that the elders are not angels. In addition, it will be noted that in verse 9 they "sang," but in verse 12, as the angels joined them, they "say." One thing that angels do not seem to do is sing, but with loud voice they praised the Lamb: "Worthy is the Lamb that was slain to receive power and riches and wisdom and might and honor and glory and blessing." Then follows an astounding occurrence that reminds us of Christ's comment in Luke 19:40 that "the stones will cry out" when every created thing (apparently including the animal kingdom) in heaven, on earth, under the earth, and in the sea (would this even include Satan and his minions?) joined the angels in recognizing God and Christ, saying, "To Him who sits on the throne, and to the Lamb, be blessing and honor and glory and dominion forever and ever."

"And the four living creatures kept saying, 'Amen.' And the elders fell down and worshiped."

THE ANTICHRIST

Before returning to earth with John in chapter 6 and the opening of the book by the Lamb, we should consider the antichrist and his reign upon earth. He plays a significant role in end time events, and his reign is ended by Christ at His second coming. The spirit of the antichrist has been present in the world throughout history and still is, as John wrote in both 1 John 2:18 and 2 John 7. That spirit is one "who denies the Father and the Son" (1 John 2:22). There will arise, however, at the end time, one who personifies this spirit and embodies all the power, authority, and even the throne of Satan himself. John is the only one who refers to this man as the antichrist; all other references to him in Scripture, and there are many, use his character to define him.

Throughout the ages, students of Scripture have attempted to identify this one who will arise at the end time. From the Middle Ages the Pope was a favorite target, and during the Reformation most of the reformers such as Luther, Calvin, Zwingli, and many, if not most, others were convinced that the papal office or the pope himself would be the antichrist. During the period of the Great Awakening in the eighteenth century, many of the leaders, including John Wesley, continued to identify the Pope. Many have had this unenviable designation over the years—such as Antiochus Epiphanes, Judas, Napoleon, Mussolini, Hitler, John Kennedy, and several others.

Apostasy and the Removal of the Restrainer

Paul told the Thessalonians in 2 Thessalonians 2:3-4 that the day of the Lord will not come "unless the apostasy comes first, and the man of lawlessness is revealed, the son of destruction, who opposes and exalts himself above every so-called god or object of worship, so that he takes his seat in the temple of God, displaying himself as being God." Paul further stated, "For the mystery of lawlessness is already at work; only he who now restrains will do so until he is taken out of the way, and then that lawless one will be revealed."

Paul went on to say in 2 Thessalonians 2:6-7, "And you know what restrains him now...until he is taken out of the way." The restrainer who would be taken out of the way has been thought to be various human agencies, such as the Roman Empire and legal systems, or spiritual agencies such as angels or the Holy Spirit. Human agencies are too weak and powerless to fight against Satan and too finite in terms of existence, for he has been restrained thousands of years. Angels appear to be restricted, for even the archangel Michael dared not judge Satan in Jude 9, but said, "the Lord rebuke you." Most Bible students today are in agreement that the restrainer is the Holy Spirit. The removal of the Holy Spirit is another indication that the rapture has taken place, since the Holy Spirit indwells believers who make up the church. If the Church is removed, the Holy Spirit as an indwelling presence will also be removed. Or expressing it another way, the Holy Spirit, as the restrainer, could not be removed without leaving the church without a Helper who, as promised by Jesus, would "be with you forever" (John 14:16). This man of sin will, therefore, not be revealed until we, the church, have been removed.

The timing of the removal of the restrainer is not indicated in this passage; however, according to Daniel 9:27, the antichrist will make a covenant with the Jews for one week (seven years), or at the beginning of the tribulation period. This action would be very evident, and would reveal his identity to Christians, if not the rest of the world. Since the antichrist is not to be revealed until some time after the restrainer is removed, it seems that the removal of the restrainer and the rapture will certainly occur before the seven-year period begins; therefore, he will not be known to the church while it is on earth. It would also seem that if this logic is sound, the expectations of the mid-trib and the post-trib believers would not be valid for they believe the church will go through either half or all of the tribulation period respectively.

The apostasy that Paul said must come first (noted above, 2 Thessalonians 2:3) is a falling away from the faith; it is not a false belief or error arising from ignorance, but is the explicit, knowledgeable rejection of Christ by those who know the truth (see also Hebrews 10:26-31).

A Look Back at Daniel's Prophecy

Although the antichrist cannot be known before the restrainer is removed, there are indications in Scripture of when the antichrist is to come, where he will come from, his nature, and the destruction, misery, and evil he will inflict upon Israel and the earth in his desire to establish himself as god. The question of when he is to come is partially answered above; that is, he will come after the removal of the restrainer and the rapture, but we are not told whether it will be soon or after a prolonged period of time. The least certain of these is where he comes from.

Nebuchadnezzar's Vision

Most believe that the antichrist will, at some time during his ascendancy to power, head up a ten-nation confederacy that will represent a revived Roman Empire. The first prophecy leading to this conclusion is Nebuchadnezzar's vision of a great statue (Daniel 2:32-45). Daniel described the statue, then told Nebuchadnezzar that he was the head of gold; the breast and arms of silver would be another kingdom inferior to his; the belly and thighs of bronze will be a third kingdom that will rule over all the earth; and the legs of iron and feet of part iron and part clay are a fourth kingdom. The feet and ten toes represent a divided kingdom that will be struck by a stone that is "cut out of the mountain without hands." That stone will crush the entire statue and will itself become a kingdom which will never be destroyed (Daniel 2:35, 44). This statue is a representation of the Gentile kingdoms that will control Israel until the stone (Christ) destroys the Gentile dominion of Israel and sets up the kingdom that will never be destroyed. It is interesting to note that the statue is seamless; there are no breaks from the head to the toes, indicating that from Nebuchadnezzar to the return of Christ there will be continuous Gentile domination of Israel. It is also interesting to note that the statue envisioned by Nebuchadnezzar, and the kingdoms it represents, appeared from the human perspective as a man—a royal figure. We will see that is not God's perspective of these coming kingdoms. But who are these kingdoms, other than Nebuchadnezzar, that Daniel refers to?

Daniel's First Vision

The next prophetic vision of the course of Gentile world dominion parallels that of Nebuchadnezzar from God's perspective. In Daniel 7:3-8, Daniel described four great beasts he saw coming up from the sea (when "sea" is used in Scripture in a generic sense, it usually refers to Gentile humanity). The first is like a lion with wings of an eagle. Its wings are plucked, and then the lion is made to stand on two feet like a man and is given a human mind. The second beast resembles a bear with three ribs in its teeth. The third is like a leopard with four bird wings and four heads. Dominion is given to the leopard. The fourth beast is not like any of the others. It is dreadful and terrifying, extremely strong with large iron teeth and ten horns. It crushes and tramples down the previous beasts and, as Daniel watched, a little horn came up among the ten and pulled three of them out by the roots. This horn has eyes like a man and uttered great boasts.

In Daniel's distress and alarm, he approached one of those standing by, and asked the exact meaning of all this, and was given the interpretation that these beasts represent four kings who will arise from the earth (Daniel 7:16-17). Most expositors agree that these four kingdoms are the same four that Nebuchadnezzar saw, but from God's perspective. Unlike the vision of Nebuchadnezzar that saw these kingdoms as glorious and together constituted a great statue, God saw them as individual ravaging beasts.

Then in 7:19, Daniel wanted to know the exact meaning of the fourth beast and its horns. He also noted that it waged war with and overcame the saints until the Ancient of Days passed judgment on the beast and the saints took possession of his kingdom. The answer came in Daniel 7:23-27. The fourth beast was a fourth kingdom and the ten horns represent ten kingdoms that will come out of it. The little horn represents another who will subdue three of the ten. The little horn (antichrist) will speak against the Most High, wear down the saints, intend to alter the times and the law, and be given "time, times and half a time" to work his will. After that, the court (described in Daniel 7:9-12) will sit to judge him. As a result, his kingdom will be destroyed and an everlasting kingdom will be established for the saints of the Highest One; all dominions will serve and obey Him (described in 7:13-14 when one like the Son of Man will be given an everlasting dominion, glory, and a kingdom that all peoples and nations might serve Him).

This vision of Daniel expands upon the vision of Nebuchadnezzar. It presents the last Gentile empire as a beast and gives a much more detailed description of its course and final destruction than that given to Nebuchadnezzar. As we have discussed, in Nebuchadnezzar's vision the last kingdom is the legs, feet, and ten toes of the statue, and these are destroyed by the striking of a stone cut without hands (the return of Christ). In Daniel's vision, the ten kingdoms arising from that beastly kingdom are represented by ten horns rather than ten toes. This vision also presents another represented as a little horn that arises out of the final ten kingdoms and takes over three of them. The vision also adds a description of some of the activities of this person which identify him as the antichrist, as we will see later.

In addition, he is given "time, times, and half a time" or three-and-a-half years to work his will. We are also given a rather interesting insight into how he will be judged—that is by a court which implies a judiciary (7:10, 26) that was probably established to administer and judge based upon God's law and not by an edict or a mandate by God. We are also told that One like the Son of Man (Christ's reference to Himself several times in the Gospels) will supplant this kingdom with an everlasting one.

But we still have not been told what nations three of these kingdoms represent. We do know from Daniel's interpretation of Nebuchadnezzar's vision that the first kingdom referred to is Nebuchadnezzar himself. In his vision he saw himself as the statue's head of gold and all of the other kingdoms were lesser than he; however, God sees this kingdom as a lion with wings of an eagle whose wings were plucked and who was given the mind of a man. This probably refers to Nebuchadnezzar's experience, related in Daniel 4:28-37. Nebuchadnezzar was glorying over Babylon, the great city he had built by the might of his power and for the glory of his majesty. Because of this display of pride, God brought him down to eat grass with the cattle. When the king's reason was restored he was humbled, realizing he was just a man. He praised God, the real Ruler of heaven and earth. So his wings (pride) were plucked and he was given the mind of a man to praise God rather than glorify himself.

Daniel's Second Vision

Daniel's next vision in chapter 8 deals with only the second and third of the subjects in the previous two visions and not the entire scope of Gentile dominion of Israel. He first saw a ram with two horns butting west, north, and south. In 8:20 he is told that the ram represented Media and Persia or the Medo-Persian Empire, which in the days of its power spread in all directions. These nations are symbolized by two horns, the longer one denotes Persia, the stronger of the two kingdoms.

Daniel then observed a male goat skimming over the earth with one conspicuous horn between its eyes that attacks the ram, breaks both its horns, and tramples it. In 8:21 he is told that the goat represents the kingdom of Greece and the horn its first king, who was Alexander the Great. Alexander established the Hellenistic or Greek empire and extended that empire around the Mediterranean Sea and to the borders of India in only twelve years. His conquests are renowned in history for their rapidity. Daniel's vision expressed this speed by reflecting Alexander's conquest of Medo-Persia as a male goat coming over the surface of the earth without touching the ground. Alexander had been tutored by Aristotle who told him he could rule the whole world if he made people adopt Greek culture. He was successful in establishing the Hellenistic culture in all those areas he conquered before he died in Babylon at the age of 33. Despite his young age, Alexander changed the course of western history. Only the Jews resisted this culture and, as we shall see, paid a heavy price. So we now have identified three of the four kingdoms that were prominent in both visions of Nebuchadnezzar and Daniel. The first was Nebuchadnezzar or Babylon; the second was Medo-Persia; and the third was Greece.

Then, in 8:8, Daniel saw the large horn of the male goat (Alexander) broken at the height of its power and in its place four conspicuous horns came up. These four horns are explained in 8:22 as four kingdoms arising in the place of the large horn, but not with his power. We know from history that after the death of Alexander, four of his generals split his empire among themselves. Cassander became king of Macedonia, Alexander's home state; Lysimachus took over Asia Minor; Ptolemy controlled Egypt; and Seleucus became king of Syria. The latter two were prominent in the control of Israel for many years. The Ptolemies were the Greek rulers of Egypt for about three hundred years and the last Ptolemaic king was Caesarion, son of Anthony and Cleopatra. As a matter of interest, Ptolemy II had the Hebrew Bible translated into Greek by seventy-two Jewish scholars for the library at Alexandria. The Seleucids were the Greek rulers of Syria for about the same period of time the Ptolemies ruled Egypt and there were several conflicts between Egypt and Syria over Israel. Under Antiochus III, the Syrians were successful in 198 B.C. in converting Israel into a Syrian buffer state.

In 8:9-14, Daniel saw coming out of one of the four horns, a little horn that grew exceedingly toward the south and east and toward the "Beautiful Land" (Israel). It grew up to the host of heaven and caused some of the host and some of the stars to fall to the earth and it trampled them down. Further, it magnified itself to be equal with the Commander of the host, removed the regular sacrifices from Him, and destroyed His sanctuary. This little horn was allowed to work its will for 2,300 days, then the holy place would be properly restored. This horn is identified as a king and further described to Daniel by the angel Gabriel in 8:23-25. He will arise in the latter period of the rule of the four kingdoms. He will be insolent (other translations say "stern faced" or "of fierce countenance"), skilled in intrigue, powerful but not by his own power, a destroyer of mighty men and the holy people. He will prosper and perform his will, magnify himself, and even oppose the Prince of princes. "He will be broken without human agency" (8:25).

According to many students of prophecy, this horn represents Antiochus IV, the great-great-great-grandson of the first Seleucus. The revealing of this person to Daniel was probably the purpose of this vision. Antiochus IV, surnamed Epiphanes (God manifest), was one of the cruelest rulers of all time and is considered to be a type of the antichrist. His aim was to unify his empire by spreading Greek civilization and culture, including religious beliefs, throughout his kingdom. He forbade the Jews, under penalty of death, to engage in their practices under Mosaic Law. Anyone caught circumcising a child, observing the Sabbath, engaging in evening and morning sacrifices, or otherwise worshiping their God would be and were put to death by the thousands. In addition, he erected an altar to the Greek god Zeus in their temple, offered swine in sacrifice, and forced Jews to participate in heathen festivities. This led to the revolt headed up by Judas Maccabeus (which is described in the books of 1 and 2 Maccabees in the Apocrypha) and resulted in the overthrow of Seleucid domination of Israel. The temple was cleansed in 165 B.C. and this cleansing is still observed and celebrated as the Feast of Lights or Hanukkah around December 25. Antiochus died, a madman, in Persia in 163 B.C.

Many expositors consider that there were two persons in view in this prophecy in Daniel 8 due to the introduction given by Gabriel in verses 17 and 19. As Gabriel began to explain the vision to Daniel, he said, "Understand that the vision pertains to the time of the end. Behold, I am going to let you know what will occur at the final period of the indignation [some translations use "wrath"], for it pertains to the appointed time of the end." This emphasis on "time of the end" indicates that the angel was not only referring to Antiochus Epiphanes but also to a similar person at the time of the end. Then in 8:25, Gabriel said, "He will even oppose the Prince of princes." This can only be Christ, but, of course, Christ was unknown at the time of Antiochus Epiphanes. It is reasonable to believe that Gabriel was speaking of both Antiochus Epiphanes and of the antichrist who will oppose Christ—indicating there is a striking similarity between the reign of Antiochus Epiphanes and future reign of the antichrist. Gabriel then closed with an instruction to Daniel: "Keep the vision secret, for it pertains to many days in the future."

Daniel and Gabriel

In Daniel 9, we read of another encounter Daniel had with Gabriel. Daniel had been in earnest prayer for the nation of Israel when suddenly Gabriel appeared to him. Daniel commented in 9:21 that "the man Gabriel, whom I had seen in the vision previously, came to me." Gabriel immediately informed Daniel that he had come, "to give you insight with understanding," and that Daniel was "highly esteemed; so give heed to the message and gain understanding of the vision" (9:22-23). This is interesting in that Daniel has had no current vision, so Gabriel must be referring to the vision that Daniel had just been considering (9:2—"the word of the LORD to Jeremiah" recorded in Jeremiah 25:11-12).

Gabriel informed Daniel about the seventy weeks, which we have already considered, so we will not go into that part of Daniel's message. I wish to consider at this point Daniel 9:26-27. In verse 26, Gabriel commented that "after the sixty-two weeks the Messiah will be cut off and have nothing, and the people of the prince who is to come will destroy the city and the sanctuary." The "prince who is to come" is considered to be the antichrist based upon the description of his activities in verse 27. The Roman Empire is considered to be the people of that prince, for they destroyed Jerusalem and the temple in A.D. 70, just thirty-plus years after the Messiah is "cut off"—referring to the crucifixion of Jesus.

Gabriel then told Daniel that this prince will make a covenant with the many (Israel) for one week (seven years). In the middle of the week, (after three-and-a-half years), he will put a stop to sacrifices and offerings (religious observances) and along with abominations (polluting the temple) will make desolate (death and destruction) until he is destroyed. This, in brief, sounds like the vision Daniel had of Antiochus Epiphanes in 8:23-26. The destruction of this prince, the antichrist, has been decreed and will be accomplished by Christ upon His return in power. This passage seems, therefore, to identify the Roman Empire as the people from which this prince will come. This last kingdom, therefore, appears to be some form of the Roman Empire, consisting of ten nations controlled by the antichrist, three of which are taken over by him. It will probably be a loose confederation, since it is described in the ten toes version as being partly iron and partly of potter's clay, that is, partly strong and partly brittle. Most expositors agree with this interpretation and refer to it as "the Revived Roman Empire."

Daniel's Third Vision

Daniel has one more vision which we need to consider in studying the antichrist, for it is the most detailed prophecy revealed to Daniel and it has several significant disclosures. It begins in Daniel 10:10-14 when an unidentified angel appeared to Daniel and indicated that he had been sent in response to Daniel's humbling himself before God, his words which were heard, and his desire to understand. He further provided Daniel with a rather unusual reason for a delay in coming to him—he had been hindered by the prince of the kingdom of Persia for twenty-one days until Michael, one of the chief princes (referred to as the "archangel" in Jude 9), came to help him. This unidentified angel was probably Gabriel, for he had come to Daniel twice before, but since he is not specifically identified I will refer to him simply as the "messenger." His struggle with the prince of Persia, who was undoubtedly a demon, gives some indication of the power of Satan and also that Satan must have a structured organization that has an administrative hierarchy, one of whom is in charge of Persia (Iran of today).

Michael, who came to help the messenger, is called one of the "chief princes" of God, which would imply that he has a significant position in God's organization. This conflict must have been an attempt by Satan's organization to prevent the angel from bringing his message to Daniel, so the message must have been deemed quite important by Satan. This scene adds a dimension to our understanding of Paul's comment in Ephesians 6:12, "Our struggle is not against flesh and blood, but against the rulers, against the powers, against the world forces of this darkness, against the spiritual forces of wickedness in the heavenly places."

The messenger then told Daniel that he had, "come to give you an understanding of what will happen to your people in the latter days" (10:14). It seems, however, that his thought was interrupted as he said that he shall return to continue the fight against the prince of Persia and the prince of Greece who was about to come, presumably to aid the prince of Persia. This is interesting in that Medo-Persia and Greece were the two major powers in the three previous visions and Greece succeeded Medo-Persia as the reigning Gentile power. The messenger seems to be somewhat preoccupied with concern about his battle with the powers of darkness, but he said, "However, I will tell you what is inscribed in the writing of truth" (some translations say "Book of Truth"). Yet again, before he continued with his message, he returned to the Persian problem as he indicated that no one stood with him against these forces except Michael, and this time he called Michael "your prince." We will see in chapter 12 how Michael fits that description.

The use of the phrase "these forces" for the princes of Persia and Greece seems to imply that the demon from Greece will join the one from Persia to contend against the messenger. It would certainly be interesting to have an insight as to how this battle was conducted. Since it was between these three beings, which I presume were indestructible, it must have been on a level other than physical. Christ used Scripture to reprimand Satan, so the Word may be a primary weapon, but then I wonder why the messenger was apparently so concerned since he was on God's side. Another matter of interest would be to know if the activities of present-day Iran (Persia) are being choreographed by this same prince. If so, will the prince of Greece again join him? These are questions that will not be answered this side of heaven, so back to Daniel.

The messenger then began his appointed task of describing the future of the Jews to Daniel. In 11:1-21, the messenger discussed the changes in the power structure of the Middle East, some of which we have already discussed relative to Daniel's previous vision in chapter 8. Persia arises and then is defeated by Alexander of Greece. There are certain intrusions by the king of the South (Egypt) and the king of the North (Syria) into each other's territories as the Ptolomies and Seleucids, who came to power from Alexander's organization, fight over Israel. The significant event from the standpoint of our study of the antichrist is in 11:21. Antiochus Epiphanes, the "despicable person," arises in Syria. He invades Egypt for the second time (11:29), but ships of Kittim (Rome) turn him back and he ends up in Israel (11:30). There "forces from him will arise, desecrate the sanctuary fortress, and do away with the regular sacrifice. And they will set up the abomination of desolation" (11:31). Verses 32-35 refer to the resistance by the Maccabees, which resulted in the defeat of Antiochus Epiphanes. Then in 11:36, the text suddenly and inexplicably turns to the king who does as he pleases and apparently has his way in whatever he undertakes. This is not Antiochus Epiphanes, but the antichrist; this is the second time that one of Daniel's vision of Antiochus Epiphanes closes by suddenly jumping thousands of years to the time of the antichrist (the other time was at the end of Daniel 8). It is interesting that both times it was a seamless transition from Antiochus to the antichrist, implying that their reigns of terror will be very similar, particularly to the Jews. Further, this may also be an indication that the antichrist has a Grecian background similar to the origin and nationality of Antiochus.

Description of the Antichrist

Daniel concluded chapter 11 with a description of some of the characteristics of the antichrist and some of the events occurring during his reign. As mentioned, he will do as he pleases, exalt himself above every god, and speak monstrous things against the God of gods. He will prosper until the indignation is finished, as has been decreed. He will show no regard for the gods of his fathers. The use of the plural words for both "gods" and "fathers" indicates that he will come from a polytheistic background, one in which his ancestors of several generations (fathers) were worshipers of many gods. The worship of many gods was the custom of most of the Mediterranean countries including Egypt, Mesopotamia (Assyria and Babylon), Canaan, Greece, and Rome at that time.

Nor will he show any regard for "the desire of women," nor for any other god; he will magnify himself above them all. The phrase, "desire of women" has been the subject of some speculation since it is not explained. Some think it refers to sexual desire and is a means of saying that he is homosexual. Others think it refers not to his sexual desire, or lack of it, but to the Jewish woman's desire to be the mother of the Messiah. If it is either one of these, it is probably the homosexual reference, since it does not seem plausible that this person is going to have any concern for the Jews, let alone such an obscure desire as that of being the mother of the Messiah. Others believe it may refer to the young god Tammuz of the Babylonians who was the husband-brother of Ishtar, goddess of fertility. Tammuz was thought to die every autumn and was restored by Ishtar in the spring, representing the crop season. The women of Jerusalem were weeping in mourning for Tammuz in Ezekiel 8:14. It should be remembered, however, that this is prophetic and is talking about a relationship at the end time; consequently, it would probably have nothing to do with concerns at Daniel's time. Since it is couched between references to the antichrist's disregard for the gods of his fathers and any other gods, the desire of women may have some religious aspect to it. It could, however, be referring to women's political, social, or legal rights, which are just coming to the fore in Arab countries. Whatever it is, the comment is indicative of a major difference between the antichrist and the women under his administration. We do know, from the text, that he will magnify himself above whatever it may be and subdue the women causing the difficulty.

He will honor a god of fortresses, which implies that he will place his faith in military strength rather than any spiritual belief, and will further honor that god by spending lavishly on military armament (11:38). This must be the god that his fathers did not know. This suggests that his fathers were not Roman for though they were into many gods, their true dependence for security was on their military, so the Romans did know the god of fortresses. The Greeks, on the other hand, were into philosophy and a hierarchy of gods which are even studied in schools in the United States today. With the exception of Alexander, they are not known as a nation with a strong military establishment, so the reference to his fathers not knowing this god could very well fit the customs of Greece. This gives more strength to the theory that the antichrist's heritage could be Greek, as was that of Antiochus. This does not rule out, however, many other Middle Eastern countries as a possible origin for the man of destruction.

Then he will "take action against the strongest of fortresses with the help of a foreign god" (11:39). The comment that he will "take action" indicates that he will do something less than attempt to make war. This could be similar to the kind of terrorism and guerrilla warfare that al Qaeda is waging against the U.S. and its allies in Iraq and Afghanistan. The term, "strongest of fortresses" fits the U.S. which is the strongest nation that has existed in the history of the world. The passage also indicates that he will have assistance from a foreign god. This is a strange comment and certainly must refer to Satan. Daniel knew that there was no other god that could really be of help, other than Satan, and Daniel had just been introduced to the power and effectiveness of Satan as the messenger had told him of his conflict with the prince of Persia.

This person gives honor to those who acknowledge him and puts them in power over "the many" (Jews); he sells land at a price to gain supporters or to enrich himself. As we consider this man, it might be useful to think in terms of Saddam Hussein to get a feel as to how a man could operate in such manner in a civilized world without anyone knowing or caring, at least for awhile. Then, at the end time (11:40), the king of the South (Egypt) and the king of the North (Syria) will come against him. He will apparently pass through several countries as he responds to this attack and one of these is the Beautiful Land (Israel). Many countries will fall, but we are not told if they are the same ones he passes through. We are told, however, that Jordan (location of Edom, Moab, and Ammon) is not one of them. We are also told that Egypt, Libya, and Ethiopia and their wealth are brought under his control.

The antichrist is then disturbed by reports from the East and North which motivate him to "go forth with great wrath" to destroy many (11:44). We are not told what these reports are about, but some believe that from the East the rumor could refer to the 200 million-man army mentioned in Revelation 9:16, and from the North possibly an invasion force from Russia (however, I do not agree with either of these contentions as will be discussed later). He then sets up his headquarters near the beautiful Holy Mountain (presumed to be Jerusalem) where it appears he will be as he comes to his end (11:45; presumed to mean death, see further discussion in chapter 13). Daniel has been given a view of the antichrist and his activities during the final days of history.

Paul provided a description similar to that of Daniel. In 2 Thessalonians 2:3-10, Paul stated that the day of the Lord will not come unless "apostasy comes first, and the man of lawlessness is revealed, the son of destruction." This one "exalts himself above every so-called god or object of worship," sits in the temple of God, and claims to be God. He is revealed when the restrainer (Holy Spirit) is taken out of the way. His coming "is in accord with the activity of Satan, with all power and signs and false wonders, and with all the deception of wickedness for those who perish, because they did not receive the love of the truth so as to be saved."

In Revelation 11, the work of two witnesses is discussed and "When they have finished their testimony, the beast that comes up out of the abyss will make war with them, and overcome them and kill them" (11:7). The beast that comes out of the abyss is the antichrist.

In Revelation 13:1-2, John added to the description of the antichrist as he described a beast coming out of the sea with the dragon (Satan) giving him his power, his throne, and great authority. One of the beast's heads was as if it had been slain and his fatal wound healed. The whole world worships this beast saying, "Who is like the beast, and who is able to wage war with him?" (13:4). He will be given authority to act for forty-two months. He speaks arrogant words and blasphemies against God, blaspheming His name and His tabernacle. He is allowed to make war with the saints and to overcome them; he is given authority over every tribe, people, and tongue, and nation. All who dwell on the earth whose names have not been written in the book of life will worship him. We will consider more on chapter 13, but for now it is a final reference to the character and activity of the antichrist.

In Summary

In order to get an understanding of the antichrist, the following points summarize what Scripture has disclosed about this person and his activity on earth during the end time (last seven years):

His name:

1   man of lawlessness (2 Thessalonians 2)
2   son of destruction (2 Thessalonians 2)
3   antichrist (1 John 2)

His authority:

1   he comes in accord with the activity of Satan with all power, signs, and false wonders and with all deception and wickedness (2 Thessalonians 2)
2   he is given the power and throne of Satan and great authority (Revelation 13)

His reign:

1   he is given time, time, and half a time (three-and-a-half years) (Daniel 7)
2   he is given authority for forty-two months (three-and-a-half years) (Revelation 13)

His revealing:

1 he will be revealed after the restrainer (assumed to be the Holy Spirit) is removed (2 Thessalonians 2)
2 the church will not know his identity because the removal of the Holy Spirit (the restrainer) implies the removal of all believers from the earth before the antichrist is revealed

His character:

1 speaks against the Most High (Daniel 7)
2 insolent, skilled in intrigue (Daniel 8)
3 shrewd, magnifies himself (Daniel 8)
4 powerful, but not by his own power; prospers and performs his will (Daniel 8)
5 does as he pleases (Daniel 11)
6 shows no regard for the gods of his fathers (Daniel 11)
7 shows no regard for the desire of women (Daniel 11)
8 exalts himself above every god (Daniel 11; 2 Thessalonians 2)
9 claims to be a god (2 Thessalonians 2)
10 speaks monstrous things about God (Daniel 11)
11 speaks arrogant words and blasphemies; blasphemes God's name and His tabernacle (Revelation 13)

His activities:

1 heads up ten kingdoms and subdues three of them (Daniel 7)
2 intends to alter time and the law (Daniel 7)
3 wages war with saints and overcomes them (Daniel 7; Revelation 13)
4 destroys to extraordinary degree, including mighty men and holy people (Daniel 8)
5 stops sacrifices and offerings (Daniel 8–9)
6 establishes a firm covenant with Israel for one week (seven years) (Daniel 9)

7 breaks that covenant in middle of week (after three-and-a-half years) (Daniel 9)

8 sets up abomination of desolation (desecration of temple) (Daniel 9, 11)

9 honors a god of fortresses, a god his fathers did not know, whom he honors with gold, silver, costly stones, and treasures (Daniel 11)

10 takes action against the strongest of fortresses with the help of a foreign god (Daniel 11)

11 honors those that acknowledge him and causes them to rule over many, and will parcel out land for a price (Daniel 11)

12 king of the South collides with him (presumably meaning Egypt attacks him, which appears to be the case since Daniel 11:42-43 says that he defeats Egypt) (Daniel 11)

13 king of the North storms against him with chariots, horsemen, and ships (king of the North is usually Syria, but due to the listed armaments, including ships, it does not seem likely in this case) (Daniel 11)

14 he takes over the treasures of Egypt; Libya and Ethiopia join him (Daniel 11)

15 apparently has conflicts with nations from the East and the North as he responds to rumors from those sources with a violent reaction (Daniel 11)

16 sits in the temple of God (indicating that the temple will be rebuilt) (2 Thessalonians 2)

17 kills the two witnesses of God (Revelation 11)

His worship by and control of the world:

18 he has a fatal wound that is healed, and the whole earth is amazed and follows after him (Revelation 13)

19 all who dwell on the earth will worship him, except those whose names are written in the book of life (Revelation 13)

20 he is given authority over every tribe, people, tongue, and nation (Revelation 13)

His demise:

1   court sits for judgment and his dominion will be taken away
    and destroyed forever (Daniel 7)
2   he is broken without human agency (Daniel 8)

As the list of disclosures is reviewed, it might occur to some that
the creation of an image of the beast and the application of mark of the
beast have been omitted. Both the image of the beast (and the worship
of that image) and the mark of the beast were instituted by the false
prophet and not by the antichrist, although it was certainly under his
authority. There may be other items which have been overlooked, but
most of the more significant attributes or activities of the antichrist have
been included and from these I have drawn certain conclusions:

1. The disclosure of the antichrist in Daniel is tied so closely to
    Antiochus Epiphanes, whose ancestors were Greek but lived
    and ruled in Mesopotamia (Syria and Babylonia) for hundreds
    of years, that I believe his nationality is probably Middle East-
    ern.
2. He is probably Muslim by religion. His religion would enhance
    his ability to effectively enter into a covenant with Israel that
    would be accepted by the Arab states, which are largely Muslim.
    The subject of the covenant is not disclosed in Scripture. It could
    be the relationship between the Jews and Palestinians that the
    United States and European allies have been trying to hammer
    out for years but have been unsuccessful in satisfying the Arabs.
    It could be related to other matters such as rebuilding the temple,
    for Daniel 9:27 says that the antichrist will stop sacrifices at the
    middle of the seven-year period (indicating that there is a temple,
    and there is no temple at the present time). He will have to be
    one who is highly respected by the Arab nations in order to get
    their agreement to such sensitive issues. The United States and
    European contingent will be pleased to have such thorny issues
    resolved.

3. The ten-nation confederacy (so-called Revived Roman Empire) that the antichrist heads up could be the Arab nations. We sometimes focus on the European Economic Community, and forget that the Roman Empire encompassed all of those countries around the Mediterranean Sea, which include most of the Arab nations. It should be noted that the Arab League, established in 1945 by the states of Iraq, Jordan, Lebanon, Saudi Arabia, Egypt, Syria, and Yemen, have since been joined by many more states—more than the necessary ten nations to create the prophesied confederacy. These nations also seem to fit the description of being partly clay and partly iron in Nebuchadnezzar's vision of the great statue in which some kingdoms will be strong and some brittle. This seems to fit these countries as they are continually in disagreement and have difficulty expressing a united front. Those three nations that antichrist will control (the little horn of Daniel 7:24) apparently are named in Daniel 11:43 as he gains control of the wealth of Egypt by force and Libya and Ethiopia follow him voluntarily. More on this and another possible ten-nation confederacy is discussed under chapter 13.

4. The Muslim Arab nations hate the Jews, as expressed by the president of Iran and reported in the *Chicago Tribune* on October 27, 2005, when he said Israel should be "wiped off the map." They would attempt to destroy the nation of Israel if it were not for the protection of the United States and European nations, particularly Great Britain. Although there is substantial anti-Semitism in Europe, it is more of an "I don't want them living in my backyard" syndrome. There is not, apparently, a desire to eliminate all Jews from the face of the earth, as it is with the Arab nations and the religion of Islam. This desire to protect Israel and return her to her land has been true for hundreds of years as evidenced by the crusades and repeated efforts to re-establish Israel as a nation, which was accomplished in 1948 with the treaty of Rome. All this to say that the antichrist, as an Arab of the Muslim religion, would have the best opportunity to establish a covenant with Israel acceptable to the Arab nations, particularly if under false pretenses and then, when it

suited his purposes, to break that agreement and pursue a policy of genocide against the Jews. "And unless those days had been cut short, no life would have been saved; but for the sake of the elect those days shall be cut short" (Matthew 24:22). Although many believe that the term "elect" refers to believers, it seems more likely to be directed to Israel, for the church will have been raptured at the time of this attempt by the antichrist to eliminate Israel.

DANIEL'S VISION AND ISRAEL

In the previous section there were substantive references to Daniel's last vision in chapters 10 through 12. Although not of importance to our understanding of the antichrist, chapter 12 provides several other disclosures to Daniel of end time events as they relate to Israel and gives us some additional information to further enhance our understanding of the end times.

As Daniel 12 opens, the messenger directed Daniel's attention to the effect of the antichrist on Israel. In verse 1, the messenger indicates that, "Michael, the great prince who stands guard over the sons of your people, will arise." But, "there will be a time of distress such as never occurred since there was a nation until that time; and at that time your people, everyone who is found written in the book, will be rescued." He also indicated there will be a resurrection, some to everlasting life and others to disgrace and everlasting contempt. So, here we find that Michael is not only a significant figure in God's hierarchy, but is also the guardian of Israel. Although we cannot draw a strong conclusion from this disclosure, it does appear, from the previous description of the messenger's battle with the prince of Persia and the prince of Greece, that nations have guardian angels that are assigned by God or Satan, as the case may be.

In Daniel 12:1 there is indication that "at that time" (presumably following on the close of chapter 11 as the antichrist comes to his end in Jerusalem), there will be a unique time of distress or tribulation such as never occurred since there was a nation, and for the first and only time in the Old Testament, the resurrection of both the righteous and the wicked is mentioned (12:2). The messenger is probably speaking only about Israel and Israel's dead regarding both resurrections, for he defined his message in 10:14 to be, "what will happen to your people [Israel] in the latter days."

The messenger told Daniel to conceal these words and seal up the book until the end time, which the angel defined as when, "many will go back and forth, and knowledge will increase" (12:4). The messenger issued two instructions to Daniel. The first was to conceal these words, presumably those the messenger had spoken to Daniel; this is much like 8:26, where Daniel was told to keep the vision secret. The second instruction was to seal up the book, presumably the one he had been explaining to Daniel, since that is the only book in view at this time, the Book of Truth. This is somewhat substantiated by their exchange in 12:8-9 as Daniel questioned, "What will be the outcome of these events?" and the messenger replied, "Go your way, Daniel, for these words are concealed and sealed up until the end time." This, in an obscure way, said to Daniel that the answer to that question is in the sealed portion of the book, and further indicates that the answer will be disclosed at the end time.

If this is the book with seven seals that Christ opens in Revelation 6, then another consideration regarding the sealed portion of the book is that it would include the disclosure of Christ's second advent and His part in the conclusion of the history of Israel and the world, and His defeat of Satan. This mystery was not to be disclosed in Daniel's time, and when it is time for disclosure, Christ will be the one to whom God will give that responsibility (Revelation 1:1). Therefore, at that time, Daniel was to receive no more information.

The event that had prompted Daniel's question was the sudden appearance of two more angels who obviously had been listening to the messenger's dissertation to Daniel. As the three angels spoke together one immediately asked, "How long will it be until the end of these wonders?" The messenger answered by raising both hands to heaven and swearing by Him who lives forever (such animation implies the messenger must have taken the question quite seriously) that it will be for time, times, and half a time (three-and-a-half years, as we have discussed before). It seems that Daniel's question ("What will be the outcome?"), the angels' question ("How long?"), and the messenger's response were referring to the same events in the undisclosed portion of the book that will result in "shattering the power of the holy people" (12:7). The messenger then concluded with a repetition of the time parameters of the last days.

From the time the abomination of desolation is set up, there will be 1,290 days (three-and-a-half years plus thirty days) (12:11) and a blessing is promised to those who keep waiting and attain to the 1,335 days (three-and-a-half years plus seventy-five days) (12:12). The difference between these two numbers of days and the 1,260 days (the Great Tribulation period; time, times, and half a time; three-and-a-half years) has been a subject of speculation among commentators, but there is no definitive answer in Scripture. The thirty days in one case and the forty-five days in the other may have something to do with Christ's return and descent from heaven or with a time of judgment. This seems to be the probable cause for the variation in days. In Revelation 13, the antichrist is given forty-two months which would use up the entire three-and-a-half-year period and then Christ will come to establish His kingdom. There would obviously be a time period required for these events, or other matters which have not been disclosed, so there is no need to speculate further. Let's return to Revelation as Christ opens the book.

REVELATION 6

The Lamb has taken the book. Then, I believe, the scene that Daniel saw and described in Daniel 7:10 takes place, "The court sat, and the books were opened." As this chapter opens, the Lamb breaks one of the seven seals and one of the four living creatures says with a voice of thunder, "Come." It is interesting to note that the book is not read or verbally explained, as was the case with Daniel's vision, but John is provided with visual scenes of the contents of the book. This is in keeping with 1:1, where God gave the Revelation to Christ to "show" to His bondservants the things which must shortly take place. So the words of the book or scroll literally come alive for John to show him those things which will come to pass.

Although the identification of the book that is in Christ's hand is not critical to understanding the scenes that John will see, it could be helpful in the enhancement of that understanding. If this is the book which Daniel was instructed to seal up until the end time, we can better reflect on some of the scenes which are shown to John as we know that they are related to Daniel's people, the Jews. I believe it is that book because, as discussed earlier, it was implied it would be sealed until the end time and there is no other book that fits that description and has been or is being revealed. I believe that if the book is from Daniel, it also answers the question debated by many scholars as to the time period incorporated in the events outlined in Revelation. Some believe that all seven years mentioned in Daniel 9:27 are included. Others believe it is only the last three-and-a-half years. As discussed previously in Daniel 12:7, the messenger answered that question rather emphatically as he raised his hands to heaven and swore by Him who lives forever that the end of these wonders, described in the sealed portion of the book, would be for time, times, and half time, or three-and-a-half years. The three-and-a-half year reference is repeated twice in Revelation, giving some credence to the assumption that this is the same book that Daniel closed.

Verses 1-2

The first scenes that develop as Christ, the Lamb, breaks the first four seals on the scroll are those commonly known as the four horsemen of the apocalypse. The horses are white, red, black, and ashen. Each has a rider who is not described other than what he is holding and what he is authorized to do. Since it is fairly clear what each of the horses and riders are authorized to accomplish, the fact that each of these actions is symbolized by a horse and rider must have some unique meaning attributable to all of them.

Horses have always been a symbol of strength and speed, and still are even in our day. We speak in terms of "horsepower" in rating engine performance, and we still enjoy seeing horses run at the Kentucky Derby and Preakness. In John's day, they were not generally useful, at least not as much as were donkeys and oxen, and were identified primarily with war in pulling chariots and mounted cavalry. In Zechariah's visions in chapters 1 and 6 of his book, they are ridden by angels who patrol the whole earth, and they symbolize speed and power. I suggest that these are the symbols they portray here. It is probable that those same angels in Zechariah's vision, who had some responsibilities regarding the patrolling and welfare of the earth, have been authorized by Christ to begin exercising judgment on Israel.

The four horsemen are apparently a unit even though each one is unveiled under a separate seal. The first is a white horse and "he who sat on it had a bow; and a crown was given to him; and he went out conquering, and to conquer." Many relate this to Christ's second coming on a white horse as described in Revelation 19, but the event we are discussing does not at all compare to that wonderful event. If the rider were Christ, I believe there would be some indication of His identity in the text; however, there is none. In addition, the events that follow the arrival of this rider—the other horses and the distress they represent—are not consistent with Christ's second advent. Some consider this to be the arrival of the antichrist, but considering this white horse to be the arrival of either Christ or the antichrist is not consistent with the riders on the other three horses. Each of the other horses represent conditions, not people, that are clearly identified as war, famine, pestilence, and death.

The rider on the white horse has a bow and yet no arrows are mentioned, indicating he represents a state of affairs in which the nations are fully armed but have not strung arrows in their bows so they are not using them for conquest. We are told that this white horse and rider went out conquering and to conquer, so apparently these conquests are accomplished politically, probably threatening the use of weapons as coercion to accomplish political goals. This might be likened to the political climate of today as a few nations, primarily the United States, are mightily armed and use the threat of that power to coerce other nations to accept or enter into desired actions. This is particularly evident today as there is military and resultant political action on many fronts such as Iraq, Afghanistan, North Korea, Lebanon, Israel, and Palestine.

The time of the white horse seems to be a time that the antichrist could arise and establish his confederacy of nations. These conditions also appear to be consistent with Daniel's vision of the antichrist discussed earlier. In Daniel 11:36-38, Daniel saw this person do as he pleases and prosper in all that he does. He honors the god of fortresses with gold, silver, and costly stones and treasures, indicating he spends great sums on weapons. It appears to be a time of comparative peace and the antichrist will add to the peace by his covenant with Israel. There currently seem to be several items on the table that could be the subject of the covenant. Several of significance at the moment are: establishing a relationship with the Palestinians; controlling Hezbollah, Hamas, and Iran; allowing Israel to rebuild the temple and renew their worship and sacrifices in the temple (as prophesied in Daniel 9:27). It may be all of the above—an exchange of land to the Palestinians for peace and the right to build the temple.

Verses 3-8

Apparently this armed, but peaceful, condition will last only until the next seal is broken. There is no mention of how long that period may last, but I believe that the white horse condition will be for a short time and may be introductory to the last three-and-a-half-year period. When the second seal is broken, a red horse comes forth and the rider is given a great sword. He is "granted to take peace from the earth, and that men should slay one another." This is, again, consistent with Daniel's vision, in Daniel 11:40-41, where the antichrist wars with the kings of both the North and the South and enters the Beautiful Land (Israel). It also follows Christ's comments in Matthew regarding wars and rumors of wars (Matthew 24:6). It may be at this time that the antichrist meets his end (Daniel 11:45), after which he recovers and is granted Satan's throne (Revelation 13:3). It is also probably at this time that he defaults on his covenant with Israel and desecrates the temple (Daniel 9:27).

The results of war are expressed by the arrival of the black horse at the opening of the third seal. This rider is given a pair of scales and a voice is heard among the four living creatures announcing extreme prices for the very basic food products. This indicates that food is scarce and there are famine conditions among the warring nations.

The fourth seal is broken and an ashen horse comes forth. This rider is named Death, and he is followed by Hades.

These four horses and riders are given authority over one-fourth of the earth to kill by sword, famine, pestilence, and wild beasts. Some commentators interpret this to mean one-quarter of the earth's population is killed by the fourth horseman. It does not say that! It says "And authority was given to them [note, "them"] over a fourth of the earth to kill with sword and with famine and with pestilence and by the wild beasts of the earth." These horses represent a complete breakdown in society as a result of war.

This brings to mind the completeness and finality of God's judgments that He expressed to Ezekiel. In Ezekiel 14:12-23, God told His prophet that not even Noah, Daniel, nor Job could deliver their sons or daughters from God's judgments of war, famine, disease, and wild beasts. These three men alone would be delivered by their own righteousness, but the country would be desolate. We can understand the desolation caused by war, which is followed by disease and famine, but what about wild beasts? This is clarified in Ezekiel 14:15, "If I were to cause wild beasts to pass through the land, and they depopulated it, and it became desolate so that no one would pass through it because of the beasts…" So we see that God would motivate the beasts to do His will. Think what terror such a situation would engender if every dog, every cat, every mouse, every bird, every cow, and all of the normally carnivorous beast were motivated to attack humans so humans would hardly be safe in their own homes.

In Ezekiel 14:21-22, God states, "How much more when I send My four severe judgments against Jerusalem: sword, famine, wild beasts, and plague to cut off man and beast from it! Yet, behold, survivors will be left in it who will be brought out, both sons and daughters." I believe this refers to the time of the four horsemen, for Jerusalem has certainly been subjected to the sword and famine, but never to wild beasts and plagues. Then in verse 23 He concludes, "For you will know that I have not done in vain whatever I did to it."

We are not told over which one-quarter of the earth these horsemen will be given authority to wreak their violence, but it appears from the Ezekiel passage that the four horsemen are directed toward Jerusalem and Israel, which will probably include the balance of the Middle East. This is consistent with the messenger's comment to Daniel that he had been sent to give Daniel an "understanding of what will happen to your people in the latter days" (Daniel 10:14).

Verses 9-11

Christ then breaks the fifth seal and the next scene shifts back to heaven. This scene is not introduced by one of the four living creatures as were the first four seals. A possible reason for this is that this seal does not introduce a judgment, and all judgments are carried out by angels under Christ's direction. John immediately sees "underneath the altar the souls of those who had been slain because of the word of God, and because of the testimony which they had maintained." Being under the altar is indication that the altar is elevated, as they quite often were. These souls have a surprising reaction as they cry out with a loud voice, presumably in unison, "How long, O Lord, holy and true, wilt Thou refrain from judging and avenging our blood on those who dwell on the earth?" Both the altar and the attitude are matters of significance.

Altars were tables or elevated platforms on which priests placed a sacrifice as an offering to God; they were used by many religions, but were of particular importance in the religious and historical life of the Jews, as they were not only used for sacrifice but also as reminders of heritage or a special event. There were two altars used in the priestly rituals of the tabernacle—the altar of burnt offering and the altar of incense. The altar of burnt offering was before the tabernacle where it was used for daily burnt offerings declaring that entry into the presence of God required a sacrificial atonement for sin (Exodus 40:29). The altar of incense was before the veil that separated the holy of holies from the rest of the worship area and continually burned incense as a symbol of prayer; it was sprinkled with the blood of the sacrificial animal (Exodus 40:26). Neither of these altars are used in the New Testament. The altar of burnt offering is no longer needed because Christ has made the full and true sacrifice. His blood covered all of our sins so the blood of animals is no longer required. "For it was fitting that we should have such a high priest, holy, innocent, undefiled, separated from sinners and exalted above the heavens; who does not need daily, like those high priests, to offer up sacrifices, first for His own sins, and then for the sins of the people, because this He did once for all when He offered up Himself" (Hebrews 7:26-27). The altar of incense was no longer needed as a symbol of prayer because Christ is now our High Priest to whom we can pray directly and "He always lives to make intercession for" those who draw near to God through Him (Hebrews 7:25).

Since the altar was of such significance to the Jews and of little importance to followers of Christ, its position in this scene strongly suggests that these are Jewish martyrs. Many, if not most, of these souls are probably those killed during the tribulation, as evidenced by their wanting revenge on those who dwell on the earth—thereby implying that those who killed them are still alive. They may be the result of those killed during the visit of the four horsemen and their judgments directed against Jerusalem and Israel.

The attitude of these souls and their appeal to God for judgment is a second indication that these are most probably Jews. They are appealing to God as did their ancestors in the Old Testament—for deliverance from and judgment on their enemies. That these souls have been saved by their belief and faith in Jesus is questionable, for as we shall see, theirs is not the attitude of those mentioned in chapter 7. It appears their presence in heaven is because of their holding to the word of God (Old Testament covenants) and their testimony regarding the word. There is no mention of Christ the Lamb.

Each is given a white robe (note—they are given robes and there is no mention of them being washed in the blood, as in 7:9-17) and told to rest a little while longer until the number of their fellow servants and their brethren who were to be killed should be completed. It is probable that the completion of this number coincides with the period of time set out in Romans 11:25, where it indicates that the Jews will continue in a partially hardened state until the "fulness of the Gentiles has come in," at which time all Israel will be saved. It does seem, by this instruction to these souls, that the tribulation is not complete and God has a predetermined number of Jews who will die during the tribulation period. However, a remnant will be saved (Daniel 12:1). It is probable that these Jewish people were saved through the promises in the Old Testament which are, of course, rooted in and fulfilled in Christ, and it may be that many of them are the prophets and saints of the Old Testament. This possibility is discussed further in chapter 16. It does seem that most came out of the tribulation period for two reasons. Their desire for revenge is focused on those living on the earth as if they were those that killed them, and secondly, they were told to rest a little while longer until an additional number of their fellow servants and brethren were killed as they were. We know any additional people killed would be killed in the remaining tribulation period.

Other observations from this passage: (1) it is fairly apparent these people are not part of the church; consequently, it should be expected that their future will be somewhat different from the church; (2) there is some indication of what we will be like in the intermediate heaven, assuming the white robes are white linen or cloth and not the white linen noted to be righteous acts of the saints (Revelation 19:8); the soul will apparently have some kind of frame or body on which to hang the robes; (3) the soul has all of the mental attributes of memory, speech, thought, as well as emotion. It seems that in the intermediate heaven we will, therefore, be much as we are on earth.

Verses 12-17

Without any preliminary announcement, John is introduced to the next scene on earth. Christ breaks the sixth seal. There was a great earthquake and the sun became black, the moon became like blood, the stars fell from the sky to the earth, the sky was split apart like a scroll when it is rolled up, and every mountain and island were moved out of their places. Just as in his day Nebuchadnezzar was used by God to administer judgment on the Jews, so in the previous seals the judgments were administered by men at the direction of God through the four horsemen. In this sixth seal, the Creator works through His creation and it appears that the whole earth and heavens are affected. If there had been any doubt about the cause of the wars and terrible times in the Middle East, there is no uncertainty regarding the cause of these phenomena. All of the powerful people—kings, commanders, great men, and the wealthy—as well as the slaves and free men, try to hide in the rocks and mountains as they prayed for those same rocks and mountains to fall on them, for they want to be hidden from God and the wrath of the Lamb. "The great day of their wrath has come; and who is able to stand?"

Students have wanted to regard these judgments as symbolic—that is, a dissolution of the present order (political, social and ecclesiastical), which may be the final result—but literal interpretation is preferred as people would not react as described in verses 15-17 to a mere breakdown in the political order.

Prophecies regarding "the day of the Lord" similar to this are found several times in Joel. The most explicit is in Joel 2:30-31, "And I will display wonders in the sky and on the earth, blood, fire, and columns of smoke. The sun will be turned into darkness, and the moon into blood, before the great and awesome day of the LORD comes." Other references in Joel to "the day of the Lord" may also be found in 2:1-2; 2:10-11; and 3:14-15. Isaiah speaks of the coming day of the Lord in Isaiah 13:9-10 as being cruel, with fury and burning anger, leaving the land in desolation as He exterminates sinners from it. The stars of heaven will not shine and the sun will be dark when it rises, and the moon will not shed its light. Amos discourages those looking forward to the day of the Lord in Amos 5:18 by saying, "Alas, you who are longing for the day of the LORD, for what purpose will the day of the LORD be to you? It will be darkness and not light." Zephaniah describes it even more dramatically in Zephaniah 1:14-15, "Near is the great day of the LORD, near and coming quickly; listen the day of the LORD! In it the warrior cries out bitterly. A day of wrath is that day, a day of trouble and distress, a day of destruction and desolation, a day of darkness and gloom, a day of clouds and thick darkness." Finally our Lord Himself described it in Matthew 24:29-30,

> But immediately after the tribulation of those days THE SUN WILL BE DARK-ENED, AND THE MOON WILL NOT GIVE ITS LIGHT, AND THE STARS WILL FALL from the sky, and the powers of the heavens will be shaken, and then the sign of the Son of Man will appear in the sky, and then all the tribes of the earth will mourn, and they will see the SON OF MAN COMING ON THE CLOUDS OF THE SKY with power and great glory.

Christ adds one rather significant point not revealed to the Old Testament prophets, which is that this event will happen immediately after the tribulation and will introduce His second coming.

REVELATION 7

This chapter is called a "parenthetical" chapter by commentators and students because it does not advance the narrative. It directs our attention to two major groups of people who are unique and quite different from one another. One is on earth and the other is in heaven. They seem to be an answer to the question asked in the last verse of chapter 6, "Who is able to stand?"

Verses 1-3

Chapter 7 begins with four angels at the four corners of the earth holding back the four winds so that no wind may blow on the earth or sea. These angels are granted authority to harm the earth and the sea and trees; therefore, the winds they are holding back are apparently God's messengers (Psalm 104:4) who carry the next round of judgments. The judgments that they are to impose are not activated, for these four angels are told by a fifth angel, who ascends from the rising sun and has the seal of the living God, not to harm the earth or the sea or trees "until we have sealed the bondservants of our God on their foreheads." There is no indication of who the "we" might be who will apply the seal, but it is probably the five angels. This scene may be the one in Daniel 12:1 which speaks of Michael, the great prince of the sons of Israel arising (note—"arising" indicates the same action as ascending), and the rescue of those Jews whose names are found written in the book.

Verses 4-8

The sealing takes place and twelve thousand from each of the twelve tribes of Israel (as named in verses 5-8), or 144,000, are sealed. In chapter 14 we are told that these are all men and the seal on their forehead is the name of both Christ and His Father. It is interesting to compare this seal which is apparently external, possibly like a tattoo as an identifier, with that of persons accepting Christ as Savior. We are sealed internally by the presence of the Holy Spirit of promise (Ephesians 1:13-14) who is not only an identifier but a helper in our daily walk and a source of wisdom in our understanding of the deep things of God. The twelve tribes listed by the angel do not include Dan of the original twelve tribes (see Genesis 49:1-28), but Dan is replaced by Manasseh, one of the sons of Joseph. Dan and Ephraim, the other son of Joseph, are not mentioned probably because they had introduced idolatry into Israel (see Judges 18:30; 1 Kings 12:28-29; Hosea 4:17).

A further glimpse of the 144,000 is provided in chapter 14. There is no indication that these are the same people who were sealed in chapter 7, but it is probably safe to assume that they are since they are also identified with a seal on their foreheads. Revelation 14 indicates why they were chosen. Apparently it was because they were "ones who have not been defiled with women, for they have kept themselves chaste. These are the ones who follow the Lamb wherever He goes. These have been purchased from among men as first fruits to God and to the Lamb. And no lie was found in their mouth; they are blameless" (14:4-5). So these Jewish men have been selected as first fruits based upon God's desire to acknowledge His chosen people and provide a cortege for Christ. They are from every tribe and they follow Him wherever He goes. Many students believe that these 144,000 were selected to preach the gospel during the tribulation period. There is no Scripture to support that supposition, and being Jews, they would not be inclined to be evangelists without a conversion experience such as Saul had on the way to Damascus (Acts 9). They may have had that experience when they were sealed or when they met Christ, but that meeting must have been in heaven, for that is where He is until His return and where they are in chapter 14. There is no record that the sealing included His anointing them on earth. There is Scripture indicating that many are saved during that time, but nothing which links these men to those who accept Christ. While still on earth after their sealing, they may possibly be witnesses to the Jewish nation that Christ is truly their King and Messiah

Verses 9-17

John next observed a great multitude from every nation, tribe, people, and tongue standing before the throne and the Lamb, clothed in white robes, carrying palm branches, and saying in loud voices, "Salvation to our God who sits on the throne, and to the Lamb." This is obviously a heavenly vision, whereas the previous one had taken place on earth. It includes angels standing around the throne, the elders, and the four living creatures. The angels all fall on their faces and worship God saying a doxology, "Amen, blessing and glory and wisdom and thanksgiving and honor and power and might, be to our God forever and ever. Amen."

One of the elders discloses to John that these people came out of the great tribulation and have "washed their robes and made them white in the blood of the Lamb." They serve God day and night in His temple. These people are quite different than those in 6:9-11. They have definitely accepted Christ as Savior and are praising Him and the Father for their salvation; they are not pleading for revenge. Their robes are white because they were washed in that precious blood of the Lamb and were not "given" to them as with those in 6:9-11. Since they came out of the great tribulation, we know that they came out of the last three-and-one-half years and we know, of course, that they are not part of the church because the church was raptured prior to the beginning of the tribulation period. We have to assume that they were either martyred or were victims of one of the judgments inflicted on the earth. Verses 16-17 promise they will no longer suffer from hunger, thirst, or heat, the Lamb will be their shepherd and God shall wipe away every tear from their eyes. They will occupy a special relationship with both the Father and the Son somewhat different than that of the church. They will serve God day and night and He will Himself perform a special, tender act as He wipes away every tear from their eyes. The Lamb shall give them special comforting as He guides them to springs of the water of life.

A WORD ABOUT CHRONOLOGY

Many commentators believe that the book of Revelation, and particularly the judgment portion (chapters 6–18), is presented in chronological order. Chapters 6 and 7, which we have just discussed, do not seem to fit a chronological pattern. In chapter 6, the great tribulation does not appear to begin until the sixth seal is broken, and yet the fifth seal discloses Jews killed during the tribulation. The four horsemen represent war, so any killed by war would not have been killed because of the word of God and their testimony.

The same is true in chapter 7: the great multitude from every nation, tribe, people, and tongue are ones who come out of the great tribulation. We know that the great tribulation is the last three-and-a-half years of history, so John was seeing the results of the great tribulation before he saw the activity of the antichrist and God's judgments during that period. It would, therefore seem that there would not be a necessity to interpret all scenes in Revelation as if they were in chronological sequence, although many of them may well be in sequence.

REVELATION 8

—❦—

Verse 1

The last seal is opened and there is silence in heaven for about half an hour. Remember, this is a scroll that Christ is unrolling and this is the last seal, so the releasing of it exposes the remainder of the scroll, which, although in written form on the front and back (5:1), is being revealed to John and probably the residents of heaven in visual form. We must also keep in mind that John is looking at events that "shall take place" (1:19), so when this last seal is released, all of the millions of those in heaven will only then understand how grievous the judgments are which will strike the earth. Their astonishment will silence them for half an hour.

Verses 2-5

The scene opens in heaven as the seven angels, who stand before God, are each given a trumpet and an eighth came and stood by the altar, holding a golden censer. After adding much incense to the prayers of the saints upon the golden altar, the smoke of the incense along with the prayers of the saints went up before God out of the angel's hand. These angels are apparently equivalent to Gabriel, for he also stands in the presence of God (Luke 1:19). The prayers of the saints are probably those prayers held by the four living creatures and the twenty-four elders in 5:8. This scene is comparable to the altar of incense, discussed earlier, in the tabernacle and the temple of the Jews on which incense was burnt and the fragrance rose to God, representing prayers of the people. The censors carried the hot coals onto which the incense was poured after the coals had been placed on the altar. Following the prayers of the saints rising to God, the angel then filled the censer with coals from the altar and threw it to the earth, resulting in thunder, lightning, and an earthquake announcing the coming judgments, apparently God's response to the intercessory prayers of the saints which rose to Him.

Verses 6-13

"And the seven angels who had the seven trumpets prepared themselves to sound them." As these angels sound their respective trumpets, the resultant judgments are devastating. Many interpret these judgments to be allegorical or symbolic; however, similar judgments outlined in the Old Testament were literal, so it would seem that God's Word is to be taken literally unless Scripture indicates otherwise. Having said that, and believing they should be taken literally, we must admit that any interpretation of these judgments is purely speculation. It does appear that the first four are almost simultaneous and are the result of objects directed at the earth from the sky, either the atmosphere or the heavens. So God, in His anger, begins directing some of His created heavens at the earth. They are also similar to the judgments God imposed on Egypt during Moses' day.

The first is a deluge of hail and fire mixed with blood that destroys one-third of the earth by burning up grass and trees. In Exodus 9:18-26, God sent a killing hail and fire that destroyed every living thing, both man and beast, that was exposed and ruined every plant and tree.

The second was something like a great mountain burning with fire that fell into the sea and a third of the sea became blood and a third of sea life died and a third of ships at sea were destroyed. This could be a huge meteor directed by God to the earth. In Exodus 7:19-24, God had Moses strike the Nile with his staff and the water turned to blood and all the fish died.

The third angel sounded his trumpet and great star fell from heaven, burning like a torch, and fell on a third of the rivers and on the springs of water. It was called Wormwood and many died because it had turned the water bitter or poisonous. Wormwood is mentioned seven times in the Old Testament, and in each case it is connected with judgment. It is only mentioned here in the New Testament, but again it is connected with judgment. It is interesting to note that the Russian nuclear plant that melted down was called Chernobyl, which means "wormwood" in Russian. In this passage, the description of the star falling from heaven is somewhat different from the mountain under the second trumpet, but it also appears that it could be a meteor, so there may be two meteors that will strike the earth in quick succession.

If these are meteors, further speculation would lead to the expectation that astronomers would be aware of them for many months and would be following their progress. The world would mount a struggle of some kind, even the launching of a nuclear device, in an attempt to destroy or divert the oncoming meteors. There would undoubtedly be other fallout from such a catastrophic event as huge tsunamis would flood coastal areas around that part of the ocean in which the first meteor fell, killing thousands and destroying cities and low-lying plains in its path.

The fourth angel sounded and one-third of the sun, moon, and stars were darkened so the day was dark for one-third of it as well as the night. The scientific community has reported that meteors have struck the earth in the long ago past and that they caused dust clouds that shut out the sun and moon for a long period of time. If the two objects that fall as a result of the second and third trumpets are meteors, the darkness may be the result of their striking the earth. Just as we would expect war to result in the effects described at the advent of the four horsemen in chapter 6 (that is, famine, pestilence, and death), so we could expect dust clouds shutting out light from the sun, moon, and stars caused by meteors striking the earth.

The first four trumpets are completed and they have brought devastation to one-third of the earth, and one-third of the oceans and rivers and even one-third of the sun, moon, and stars were affected. We are not told the boundaries of the one-third of the earth that has been affected, but it has probably been that third of the earth that includes Israel and the Middle East.

Since the first four trumpet judgments of chapter 8 were directed at the earth and sea, it seems that they may have been the winds, or judgments, the four angels in chapter 7 were holding back and were instructed not to harm the earth or the sea or the trees until the 144,000 had been sealed.

The final scene in chapter 8 is an eagle announcing the remaining three judgments that are to be so terrible that he cries out, "Woe, woe, woe to those who dwell on the earth."

REVELATION 9

Verses 1-2

The fifth angel sounded his trumpet, and a star which had fallen from heaven to earth at some previous time was given the key to the bottomless pit. Although we are not told who the star is, it is probably Satan or one of his angel-demons. That the star is a male is evident, for in verse 2 it says that "he opened the bottomless pit." There are Scriptures that seem to reference the fall of Satan from heaven. In Isaiah 14:12 it seems to refer to the fall of Satan from heaven and he is called "star of the morning." This is not a clear reference, but many commentators consider it possible that it did refer to Lucifer, even though the rest of that chapter is clearly in reference to the king of Babylon. The lamentation over the king of Tyre in Ezekiel 28 is thought to be a clear reference to Satan's fall; however, there he is not referred to as a star. And then Christ comments in Luke 10:18 that He saw "Satan fall from heaven like lightning." Revelation 12:4 refers to the tail of the dragon sweeping one-third of the stars of heaven to earth, and then 12:7-9 indicates that the dragon is Satan; he was thrown down to earth and his angels were thrown down with him. We know, therefore, that Satan did fall from heaven and other angels fell with him. The star referred to in verse 1 must, therefore, be Satan or one of his most highly placed angel-demons for him to be given the key to the bottomless pit. We are not told who gave him the key, but it must have been allowed by God.

The bottomless pit or abyss should be translated literally as "shaft of the abyss" (according to a note on verses 1 and 2 in the NASB Study Bible). It is probably not Hades for Christ has that key (Revelation 1:18). In Luke 8:31, the demons that Christ exorcised out of the man who called himself Legion entreated Him not to send them to the abyss; instead, they asked to enter the herd of pigs. Apparently the abyss had a fearful reputation among demons, so it must also be a place of imprisonment for certain select ones. First Peter 3:19-20 indicates that those imprisoned, presumably in the abyss, were those who were disobedient in the days of Noah, and Christ went and made proclamation to them after His crucifixion. This proclamation was probably a statement of His victory and not of forgiveness. We are also told in Jude 6, "And angels who did not keep their own domain, but abandoned their proper abode, He has kept in eternal bonds under darkness for the judgment of the great day." These are, apparently, the same ones spoken of by Peter; their place of detention is the abyss. We know, both from Scripture and the testimony of missionaries and others in our own day, demons are currently active in the world, so evidently all fallen angels are not now imprisoned. Apparently, all other disobedient angels who did not indulge in the grievous sin (some believe mating with humans—see Genesis 6:2) were left free to serve Satan, their king. The giving of the key to either Satan or one of his angel-demons is certainly an illustration of how God restrains and controls Satan—he is allowed to do only those things that God permits.

Verses 3-6

Satan or one of his demons opens the bottomless pit with the key releasing smoke like a great furnace that is so dense it blots out the sun. Out of the smoke locusts came forth and the power of earthly scorpions was given to them. They were to use this power to sting people, inflicting painful wounds like a scorpion, but they were not to harm any green plants, trees, or the people who had the seal of God on their foreheads. These must be the 144,000 who were sealed in chapter 7, for they are the only ones whom Christ has revealed to have been sealed. The locusts have the power in their tails to hurt people for five months, which is the normal life span of locusts (from May to September). Locusts normally eat vegetation as did those sent by the Lord against Egypt in Moses' day (Exodus 10:1-20), but these cannot harm any of the earth's vegetation. On the other hand, locusts do not normally have the power to sting and hurt people, but these are released for that purpose. Because of the sting people want to die, but cannot.

Verses 7-12

A most interesting aspect of the locusts is their appearance, in which there seems to be no purpose other than to be somewhat frightening (however, their sting would be of enough concern to attempt to avoid them at all cost). Apparently, they were the same size as present-day locusts or as we know them—grasshoppers. As a child I observed many grasshoppers in my grandfather's cornfield and, as I recall them, their appearance was somewhat similar to John's description. He tells us that the ones he sees are like horses prepared for battle, with what appeared to be crowns of gold on their heads (more likely gold bands). They had faces like men, hair like women, and teeth like lions. They had tails like scorpions, presumably curved and arching over their backs. Those characteristics were unique to John's locusts, as the ones I remember seeing had only long faces that looked more like horses than people. Finally, John's locusts had breastplates that looked as if made of iron. The sound of their wings was like chariots and horses going into battle. Some commentators have attempted to cast meaning to each of these physical characteristics—such as the face of a man indicates intelligence and the hair of a woman seductiveness—but I believe any such conjecture is of little value.

The locusts have a king over them, the angel of the abyss, who is given a name both in Hebrew, *Abbadon*, and in Greek, *Apollyon*. Both of these names mean destroyer. The fact that they have a king indicates they are demonic beings, for as it says in Proverbs 30:27, "The locusts have no king, yet all of them go out in ranks." Since this angel is given a name and is not identified as Satan, the angel is probably one of the highest-ranking angel-demons in Satan's hierarchy. Since these are demonic spirits, they would not be seen by humans any more than the four horsemen can be seen by anyone other than John, who is seeing them through the eyes of God. God sees the demons for what they are and He allows them to inflict some form of painful boils or infections on people, similar to the plague of boils inflicted upon the Egyptians and their animals (Exodus 9:8-12). This is evidence, once again, that God controls Satan and his minions—they are only allowed to relate to humans as God gives them permission.

"The first woe is past; behold, two woes are still coming after these things."

Verses 13-21

The sixth angel sounded, and a voice from one of the four horns of the golden altar before God tells the sixth angel to release the four angels that are bound by the Euphrates River. These four angels have been prepared for this very hour, day, month, and year to kill one-third of mankind. The instructions for this judgment come from the golden altar before God's throne on which the prayers of all the saints had been laid (8:3). The prayers of those Jews who had been killed and whose souls were under the altar calling out for revenge in 6:9-10 were certainly part of the prayers on the altar. Now God begins to answer those prayers with instructions coming directly from His altar.

His servants who will impose this judgment are the angels that have been bound for this purpose at some time in the past. Having been bound would imply that these must be some of those who fell with Satan. God uses angels of Satan to accomplish His purpose. The fact that these angels had been bound is again an example of God's restraining hand on the activities of Satan and his angels and further evidence that the restrainer referred to in 2 Thessalonians 2:7 is the Holy Spirit. It is also interesting to note in this passage the exact timeliness of God's purposes. They were prepared for this very hour. This may not be evidence that all future events are on a specific schedule, but it appears all major activities are planned and scheduled in advance by God.

Verse 15 indicates that the objective and purpose of the release of these four angels is to kill one-third of mankind. We are not told how many that might be. Consider that the church has been raptured; many more were killed when the four horsemen were given authority over one-fourth of the earth; many died from the poisoned water after Wormwood fell; and many died from the falling meteors. If there are approximately 6 billion people on earth today, and if we assume that these events take about one-third or 2 billion (and I have no idea if that is at all close) then there would still be 4 billion, of which one-third would approximate 1.3 billion. Whatever the number, this judgment will kill more people than have died in all the wars the earth has sustained throughout history.

Without explanation, John states in verse 16 that he hears that the number of armies (note that the word "armies" is plural) of the horsemen was 200 million, but he does not indicate who told him. It appears that these armies (that have certain qualities similar to the demons coming out of the pit under the fifth trumpet) are the resources that will be used by the four angels to kill one-third of mankind. John sees in the vision the horses and riders and describes the breastplates of the riders and the heads of the horses, which are like the heads of lions, with fire, smoke, and brimstone coming out of their mouths. The power of the horses is in their mouths and their tails. Their tails are like serpents whose heads can do harm. According to verse 18 the four angels accomplished their goal as "a third of mankind was killed by these three plagues, by the fire and the smoke and the brimstone, which proceeded out of their mouths." There have been several interpretations of these armies, but again, each is purely speculation. There is some question whether this should be taken literally. To move such armies would be almost impossible with or without transportation, and there certainly would not be 200 million horses available. In the mid-1990s, the horse population of the world was estimated to be only 60 million.

Others believe that these armies are related to Revelation 16:12, where the pouring out of the sixth bowl dries up the Euphrates to make way for the kings of the east. Similarly Daniel 11:44 speaks of the antichrist hearing rumors from the East. Both of these passages infer that there will be some kind of invasion toward Israel from the eastern nations during the time of the antichrist—many suggest from China. If this is the correct interpretation, then the chronology of Revelation is again in question as the sixth bowl should precede the sixth trumpet if drying up the Euphrates is of any value to the armies. Some believe the rather awesome description of this great force could be John's view of what we know as modern warfare with much mechanized equipment and vehicles seemingly spouting fire and brimstone. But, here again we have a problem with numbers—there would not be sufficient trucks, tanks, and other vehicles to transport 200 million men, nor the roads on which to move them from China to the Middle East.

It is interesting to note that John ascribes all of the destruction and death to the horses and none to the riders. Verse 18 indicates that one-third of mankind are killed by these three plagues of fire, smoke, and brimstone. The use of the word *plagues* implies disease rather than battle wounds. It is, of course, impossible to identify this judgment and those who carry it out, but when we consider that the armies were apparently released under the auspices of the four bound angels, that they are to kill one-third of mankind (which could be over one billion people), that they are described as delivering three plagues, that their description is like that of the demons under the fifth trumpet, and that (although this passage does not indicate timing, based upon the timing of the tribulation period the killing must be completed within a rather narrow window of time), it does seem probable that they are inhuman destroyers and disease is their weapon.

It would be unlikely that human armies could kill over one billion people in a relatively short period of time unless they were to release nuclear devices over most of the planet and particularly into areas where large numbers of people live (such as China and India). Armies of 200 million demons released into the world could very well deliver plagues all over the world within a short time. As with the locust plague, if these are demons, they would not be visible to the earthly population. If such an unusual "horse" and rider were visible, people would be terrified by both their size and their destructive power, and would certainly realize they were demons. That would, I believe, pretty well discourage the continued worship of demons, but as verses 20 indicates, "the rest of mankind, who were not killed by these plagues, did not repent." Such worship continued. If they were unseen, people would consider the plagues as natural events and not attributable to demons (as with the AIDS epidemic) and would continue to worship demons and idols—"they did not repent of their murders nor of their sorceries nor of their immorality nor of their thefts"—just as today people do not turn to God because of war or disease.

Mankind is not changed by punishment but only through Christ's work in their hearts and lives. Only demons believe and shudder (James 2:19)!

REVELATION 10

A parenthetical passage occurs from 10:1–11:14. The narrative is not advanced, but other matters are presented that contribute to the total prophecy. As this parenthesis occurs, there have been seven seals and six trumpets, and the seventh trumpet is about to sound.

Verses 1-4

As chapter 10 opens, John sees another strong (some translations say "mighty") angel coming down out of heaven, clothed with a cloud, a rainbow upon his head, a face shining as the sun, and feet like pillars of fire. Some believe this is Christ due to his appearance. Christ did appear as an angel of the Lord or God in the Old Testament. He appeared to Hagar in Genesis 16:7, to Abraham in Genesis 22:11; to Jacob in Genesis 31:11, and to Moses in Exodus 3:2-6. There were many more appearances, or "epiphanies," in the Old Testament. However, He is never described as appearing as an angel after His resurrection. It may also be noted that this angel came to earth from heaven and, as far as we know, Christ will only make this descent at the time of His second coming. John had seen a strong angel in 5:2, but apparently it was not the same one, for he says that this is "another" one. This must be an exceptional angel both in size and in appearance, which John describes in some detail.

This angel has one foot on the land and one on the sea. Although this stance could be achieved by just standing on the seashore with one foot in the water and one on the shore, the way John describes his posture, however, leaves the impression that the angel was quite large. His size is further emphasized as his shout is like a lion's roar, and it is answered by seven peals of thunder. The thunder obviously expressed some idea or statement because John was about to write down what he had heard when he was told not to write what the thunder had spoken. This obviously leaves us to wonder what magnificent or mysterious words had been delivered to John that he could not divulge.

Verses 5-7

The angel prefaced an announcement by swearing by Him who lives forever and ever, who created heaven and earth and everything in them (indicating God's special relationship and authority over the earth as its Creator), "that there shall be delay no longer." It appears at this point that God has allowed Satan to release all of his demons on the earth so that his kingdom has been realized and is fully operational. This angel is probably not visible nor his message audible to inhabitants of earth, so his task is to act as an intermediary between God and Satan. He has come, as would a Secretary of State from one nation to another, to announce the claim and right that God has upon the earth. He delivers the message to Satan and his kingdom that, under this claim and right, there would no longer be a delay in the judgments and destruction that are about to fall. Satan would of course be fully aware of creation and God's right to take back His creation at any time. Verse 7 indicates that when the seventh angel sounds his trumpet the mystery of God is finished, as He preached to His servants the prophets.

What is this mystery that He preached to His prophets? The answer seems to appear in 11:15 as the seventh angel sounds and loud voices in heaven announce that "the kingdom of the world has become the kingdom of our Lord, and of His Christ; and He will reign forever and ever." A review of the many prophecies in the prophetical books of the Old Testament indicates that the restoration of Israel as a nation is by far the most-mentioned prophecy and, in many of those instances, the establishment of righteousness, of God's dwelling place, and of His kingdom are also emphasized. So the "mystery of God" is the restoration of Israel and the establishment of His kingdom.

These two themes are developed in several passages of Scripture. Jeremiah 3:17 says that "at that time they shall call Jerusalem 'The Throne of the LORD,' and all the nations will be gathered to it, to Jerusalem, for the name of the LORD; nor shall they walk anymore after the stubbornness of their evil heart." In Ezekiel 43:7, God says to Ezekiel, "Son of man, this is the place of My throne and the place of the soles of My feet, where I will dwell among the sons of Israel forever." There are too many prophecies relating to the restoration of Israel to mention, but a few include: Isaiah 11:1–12:6; Isaiah 25:1–27:13; Isaiah 43:14-28; Isaiah 60–63, Isaiah 66; Jeremiah 30:1-11; Ezekiel 11:16-20; Ezekiel 20:34-44; Ezekiel 28:25-26; Ezekiel 34:11-31, Ezekiel 37:1-23 (the famous passage of the valley of dry bones and graves, which is the Jewish nation and the nations from which they come); Hosea 2:18-23; Zechariah 2; and Zechariah 8.

The second coming of Christ, which is the foundation of the kingdom, is also prophesied in an obscure way in Ezekiel 34:23-24 and 37:24-25 as "David" is to reign over Israel forever. Many believe this reference is really to Christ; since His name was not known in the Old Testament and since He is to fill the throne of David (Isaiah 9:6-7), He is referred to as David. Christ is also referred to as the Lord who will go forth and fight against the nations and "His feet will stand on the Mount of Olives" which "will be split in its middle from east to west" (Zechariah 14:3-4). He will come with all the holy ones with Him, "and the LORD will be king over all the earth; in that day the LORD will be the only one, and His name the only one" (Zechariah 14:9). Finally the defeat of the antichrist, which is necessary for the establishment of God's kingdom, is mentioned in Daniel 7:11, after the beast was judged, he was slain and his body destroyed by fire.

In summary, it appears there are four major prophecies preached by God to the prophets—all of which come to pass almost simultaneously at the end time:

(1) Christ returns in power judging the nations.
(2) Christ defeats and destroys the antichrist.

(3) Christ controls the earth and establishes His kingdom in Jerusalem.

(4) Israel's return to the promised land is permanently and fully accomplished as they acknowledge Him as the Messiah and Savior.

Christ also defeats Satan, but that is not mentioned specifically in these Old Testament prophecies. It is certainly implied, however, for Christ could not establish His kingdom if that were not so.

Verses 8-11

In verse 2 it is noted that the strong angel has in his hand a little book that is open. Those who believe this angel is Christ also believe that the book is the book that Christ took from God in chapter 6 and it is now open because the seven seals have been removed. It is, however, called a "little book," which seems to distinguish it from the one Christ opened in 6:1. A voice from heaven tells John to take the book, which he does. As he does, the angel tells him to eat the book, and that it will taste sweet but will make his stomach bitter, and it does. The angel then tells John he must "prophesy again concerning many peoples and nations and tongues and kings." It is interesting to note that John is interactive with the vision as he talks with the angel and takes the book from him. This is not the first time he has interacted with the vision. In 5:5, John was comforted by one of the elders when he was in tears. In 7:14, one of the elders answered his question about who the great multitude represented. This interactivity would indicate that John's comment in 1:10 that he "was in the spirit on the Lord's day" meant more than being in a trance-like state during which he had a vision or dream. Instead, it appears that he somehow experienced those things that he saw and, in a manner of speaking, moved forward in time or to another dimension to observe the actual occurrence. How? I don't know, of course, but we do know he observed things taking place, and then in these three cases was able to integrate with the action that was going on and participate at some level.

John was told to eat the book, which he did, just as Ezekiel had done in his day (Ezekiel 3:1-3). The purpose was so he would fully absorb its contents and understand what God had to say about those things that would otherwise be a mystery to him. It would seem that God is speaking to Israel because the Jews, in particular, would be aware of this manner of receiving the word of God, for they were familiar with Ezekiel's experience. The book is a "little book" and John is told that the message contained in it is sweet to the taste, but bitter to the stomach—good news and bad news. After eating the book, he is told to "prophesy again concerning many peoples and nations and tongues and kings" (10:11), presumably using the influence of the book he has eaten. Based upon John's disclosures in the final chapters of Revelation, the book would seem to contain the substance of God's relationship with the antichrist and Satan during the final days, the last three-and-a-half years of the tribulation period. The good news is about Christ's triumphant return and the setting up of His kingdom. The bad news that sours the stomach is the tribulation that must still be endured by Israel and the world prior to Christ's return.

.

REVELATION 11

According to many scholars, chapter 11 is one of the most difficult chapters in Revelation. As might be anticipated, there is wide disagreement as to the interpretation of the chapter. There are a couple of things to keep in mind as this chapter is considered. First, the chapter is definitely directed to the Jews and, although it begins with reference to the temple, there was no temple when John wrote. John was writing this book toward the end of the first century after the Roman Emperor Titus had destroyed Jerusalem and burned down the temple in A.D. 70. The first word to begin the chapter is "and" in an earlier version of the NASB and "then" in the most recent version of the NASB. In either case, the word ties chapter 11 to chapter 10 and thereby indicates that it is included in the parenthetical passage beginning at chapter 10:1 and running to 11:14. So we should read the beginning of chapter 11 as a continuation of chapter 10.

Verses 1-2

After John had eaten the little book (10:10), he was told he must prophesy concerning many peoples and nation and tongues and kings. In 11:1, he was given "a measuring rod like a staff; and someone said, 'Rise and measure the temple of God, and the altar, and those who worship in it." But, he was told, "Leave out the court which is outside the temple…for it has been given to the nations; and they will tread under foot the holy city for forty-two months," which is the familiar three-and-a-half years we have considered several times, the time period known as "the great tribulation."

John has again been drawn into active participation in his vision. Why was this unusual instruction given to him? And why is there no indication of whether he did as he was instructed? If he had made the measurements, wouldn't we have been told the results? Some commentators believe this was God's way of identifying the temple as His special property; His knowing that the antichrist was to desecrate the temple served as a warning that there would be a judgment for doing so.

I don't believe the measuring was necessary to identify the temple as God's property; it was more likely that the instruction was given to John to serve as both a reminder and an encouragement to the Jewish nation. Because John is asked to measure the temple means there will indeed *be* a temple. The Jews had been promised a rebuilt temple during Ezekiel's day; that temple would be built and with it would also come the glory of God to live with them once again. John's measurements would merely confirm that the rebuilt temple is truly the one promised Ezekiel, which he had recorded centuries earlier. There would be no need to give John's measurements here for that would only repeat Ezekiel's detailed description.

In Ezekiel 37:27-28, the Lord said that he would dwell with Israel forever and that His sanctuary would be in their midst forever. Ezekiel then had a vision beginning in 40:2. God brought him to a high mountain. There, a man, whose appearance was like bronze, appeared with a measuring rod in his hand. This man proceeded to measure and describe in detail the floor plan of a temple, and Ezekiel recorded everything (Ezekiel 40:5–43:17). However, that temple has never been built even to this day. (Three temples have been built in Jerusalem—the first by Solomon, the second by Zerubbabel, and the third by Herod, but all of these had different floor plans than the one described by Ezekiel.) In Ezekiel 43, the prophet watched the glory of the Lord return to the temple: "I looked, and behold, the glory of the LORD filled the house of the LORD" (44:4). Recall that this reversed what had occurred in Ezekiel 9–10 where Ezekiel had watched as the glory of the Lord departed from the temple because of the sins of the people. God says of the newly-built temple, "This is the place of My throne and the place of the soles of My feet, where I will dwell among the sons of Israel forever" (43:7).

It seems that the instruction to John to measure the temple may have been to remind the Jewish nation of that previous promise and to show that this temple that John was measuring is the fulfillment of that promise. If that is indeed the case, it would also be a notice of the soon return of God's glory—for it was to this temple that Ezekiel had seen His glory return. We are not told when it is to be rebuilt, but it may be during the first three-and-a-half years of the tribulation period before the covenant is broken by the antichrist (according to Daniel 9:27).

Verses 3-4

Without introduction or explanation, John continues with words that presumably are a continuation of the voice of that "someone" who instructed him to measure the temple. The statement begins with "I" and continues "will grant authority [some translations say "power"] to my two witnesses, and they will prophesy for twelve hundred and sixty days, clothed in sackcloth." It is interesting to note that the translators did not capitalize the word "my," which they would have done if they had attributed this statement to the Father or Christ. But if God is not the "someone" who is speaking, then who is this speaker who could grant them authority and could call them "my two witnesses"? The one who granted this authority and the promise to perform as they did could have been an angel, but it seems more likely to have been God.

Next, John is told that "these are the two olive trees and the two lampstands that stand before the Lord of the earth." What was the speaker trying to tell John with this information? Possibly it was a reference to something that was expected to be familiar to John (or to the readers of the passage) that would give him some idea as to who these two witnesses might be.

Some students believe that the two witnesses were Elijah and Enoch because neither one of them died. In 2 Kings 2:11, Elijah was taken up by fiery horses and a chariot while talking to Elisha. In Genesis 5:24, it is recorded that "Enoch walked with God; and he was not, for God took him," indicating that, like Elijah, Enoch was taken to heaven without dying. Others believe the two witnesses are Moses and Elijah because (1) in their Old Testament roles, they were servants of the Lord in dispensing judgments; (2) their powers were similar to the powers that these two witnesses will display during their short time on earth; and (3) they were both with Christ on the Mount of Transfiguration. It seems that if God was concerned about letting us know who these men were because it would enhance our understanding of the passage, He would have told us. Instead, He informed us only of their relationship to Him.

The speaker calls these two witnesses, "two olive trees and the two lampstands that stand before the Lord of the earth." Again, we turn our attention to the Old Testament where Zechariah had a vision and saw "a lampstand all of gold...also two olives trees by it" (Zechariah 4:2-3). Apparently Zechariah either was not curious as to what the lampstand represented, or possibly he knew that it was a picture of God's witness in the world. In Zechariah's day that witness to the world was to come through Israel; in our time, it comes through the church (as we saw in Revelation 1). When Zechariah expressed his curiosity about the two olive trees, however, the angel avoided an answer. Instead, he told Zechariah that this was a message from the Lord to Zerubbabel—that he was to rebuild the temple. In Zechariah 4:6, Zerubbabel was encouraged that he would accomplish that task "'not by might nor by power, but by My Spirit,' says the LORD of hosts." In other words, Zerubbabel did not have the power of Solomon and could not command that the temple be rebuilt, but with the Lord's help, he could get it done.

Then Zechariah's question became more specific. Instead of asking about two olive trees, he referred to the two olive branches that were beside the two golden pipes. The angel, who had not answered Zechariah the first nor the second time he had asked about the olive trees, answered quickly when he was asked about the branches. This may have been because of the Lord's discussion with Joshua, when He told Joshua He was going to bring in His servant, the Branch, the Anointed One—a reference to Christ (Zechariah 3:8-9). The angel then identified the branches of the two olive trees Zechariah saw in verse 3 as "the two anointed ones, who are standing by the Lord of the whole earth" (Zechariah 4:14). In Zechariah's case, these were Joshua and Zerubbabel, who were to rebuild the temple. The olive trees provide a continuous supply of oil through the branches to the lampstand. This represents the Holy Spirit and His continuous administration and filling to the anointed ones of God.

Therefore, in Revelation 11, the two olive trees represent the continuous supply of oil (Holy Spirit) to empower the two lampstands (the two witnesses) to prophesy and to employ the defensive and offensive weapons God has provided to them. They prophesy in the tradition of the Old Testament prophets, in sackcloth and ashes signifying repentance, for 1,260 days (three-and-a-half years). We are not told what their message will be, but I don't believe their dress, their power, and their defense system are compatible with a message of love or grace. The message will be one of God's holiness, power, and judgment, somewhat like that of the Old Testament prophets. I believe they will call the Jews to repentance and admonish them for the sins of their fathers, and will also include a message for the antichrist regarding the judgment soon to befall him and his followers.

Verses 5-6

The two witnesses will have a deadly defense system; they cannot be killed until their time is up (after three-and-a-half years). Anyone who even desires (Scripture uses "desires," which indicates having only the thought) to harm them will be killed by fire coming out of the witnesses' mouths. In addition, during this time, the two witnesses will also have the power to smite the earth with plagues; they can shut up the sky (cause drought), turn waters into blood, and "smite the earth with every plague, as often as they desire." Clearly, these men are given amazing powers.

Verses 7-10

When they have completed their testimony at the end of three-and-a-half years, the beast out of the abyss will make war with them and kill them. The description of the beast out of the abyss (in 17:8) leads us to believe that it is the antichrist who will kill them. Their dead bodies will lie in the street of the city "which mystically is called Sodom and Egypt, where also their Lord was crucified" (obviously referring to

Jerusalem). The comment that the beast makes war with them indicates that the two witnesses will put up some kind of battle and will not just be killed in cold blood.

The witnesses were speaking of God's judgment as God continued to reach out to His people—just as He had through the Old Testament prophets. It is apparent from the celebration the people will have after the deaths of the witnesses that they did not listen; the Jews will treat these two prophets just as they treated the Old Testament prophets. Israel's continued disbelief and apostasy was likened to adultery in the Old Testament. In Jeremiah 23:14, God said, "Also among the prophets of Jerusalem I have seen a horrible thing: The committing of adultery and walking in falsehood…All of them have become to Me like Sodom, and her inhabitants like Gomorrah." In Ezekiel 23, God presented His view of Israel's idolatry and apostasy referring to her harlotries with many nations, including Egypt.

The bodies of the two witnesses lay in the street of Jerusalem, where, I believe, they had spent the entire three-and-a-half years proclaiming their message. Leaving the bodies unburied would be obscene to the Jews; this action reflects the utmost hatred and disrespect of the witnesses and the Jews by the antichrist and those who follow him. The rest of the world is able to observe their dead bodies (through television or the Internet, I assume), and further reveals the hatred of the witnesses by rejoicing at their death, using it as an occasion to celebrate and send gifts to one another. This gives us some idea of the message delivered by the two witnesses—it certainly was not a popular one when people all over the world are so happy that they have been silenced. But then again, the messages brought by the Old Testament prophets weren't popular either.

Verses 11-14

After three-and-a-half days, however, the Lord will raise the dead bodies of the witnesses, much to the distress and fear of those watching. When they hear a loud voice from heaven say, "Come up here," the dead witnesses will come back to life and rise up to heaven in a cloud. That very hour there will be a great earthquake that will kill seven thousand people and destroy a tenth of Jerusalem. Those watching will be terrified and give glory to God—apparently in response to the message they had been hearing from the witnesses, as well as from their fear when they see the dead bodies come back to life and witness the earthquake. These people will include the Jewish inhabitants of Jerusalem, and it is interesting to observe that they will recognize and give glory to God but they do not yet recognize their Messiah, the Lord Jesus.

There are certain references of particular interest in this chapter. In verse 2, the nations were given forty-two months (three-and-a-half years) to control Jerusalem, which indicates that this time period is the last half of the seven-year period of tribulation referred to by Daniel. At the end of that period, the antichrist will be defeated and his kingdom will be destroyed forever (Daniel 7:25-27), thereby ending the nations' control of Jerusalem.

In verse 3, the two witnesses are given 1,260 days (three-and-a-half years) to prophesy. Apparently this will be during the same period of time given the nations in verse 2.

In verse 7, the beast that comes up out of the abyss will kill the witnesses. This raises two points. First, the beast coming out of the abyss is not mentioned until 17:8, where it states that "he is about to come up out of the abyss," so apparently he had not yet made an appearance in chapter 11. Presumably he has to come out of the abyss in order to wage war with and kill the two witnesses in chapter 11. If so, these scenes are not chronological; instead, the scene in chapter 11 will come after the scene in chapter 17. Second, if both the nations and the two witnesses are given exactly three-and-a-half years, then the last judgments (which we will consider after the seventh trumpet is sounded) must be after this three-and-a-half-year period is finished, for the seventh trumpet is sounded after the two witnesses are raised to heaven. That may account for the extra thirty and seventy-five days, respectively, that were mentioned in Daniel 12:11-12.

This parenthetical passage that began at 10:1 closes here at 11:14. The second woe is past and the third is coming quickly.

Verses 15-19

The seventh angel sounded his trumpet and loud voices sounded in heaven, saying, "The kingdom of the world has become the kingdom of our Lord, and of His Christ; and He will reign forever and ever." The twenty-four elders who sit on thrones before God (we first met them in 4:4), fell on their faces and worshiped God. They thanked and praised Him because He had taken His great power and begun to reign.

According to verse 18, the nations were enraged and God's wrath came (the seven bowls), followed by the time for the dead to be judged and the time for God to reward His bondservants, the prophets, the saints, and those who fear God's name, and to destroy those who destroy the earth.

Then John observed a marvelous sight as "the temple of God which is in heaven was opened; and the ark of His covenant appeared in His temple, and there were flashes of lightening and sounds and peals of thunder and an earthquake and a great hailstorm." Notice that this is the temple of God in heaven. I believe that the ark is the same one that was the center of worship and the symbol of His presence among the Jewish people for many years. It has been the "lost ark" since the temple was destroyed by the armies of Nebuchadnezzar in about 586 B.C. If this is that ark and not a heavenly replica, then God must have taken it to heaven for His temple there.

The seventh trumpet appears to embody the seven bowls and the sounding of that trumpet releases those bowls of God's wrath. The twenty-four elders summarize the effect of the release of the bowls in their prayer of thanks for the arrival of the kingdom of the Lord and His Christ with its concomitant effect on the earth's inhabitants. The nations are enraged, a fulfillment of the prophecy in Psalm 2:2-9 wherein the nations want to throw off the shackles imposed by His Anointed One. It is also time for the dead to be judged (Revelation 20:11-15), possibly a fulfillment of the prophecy that was spoken of by Daniel regarding his people, the Jews, that "many of those who sleep in the dust of the ground will awake, these to everlasting life, but the others to disgrace and everlasting contempt" (Daniel 12:2).

It is also time "to reward your bondservants the prophets and the saints and those who fear your name." Here we have designated references to prophets (Daniel 9:6; Amos 3:7), saints (Daniel 7:22), and those who fear God (Psalm 111:10; 112:1) that are Jewish in nature. The rewards are associated with the arrival of Christ and the establishment of His kingdom on David's throne. They are bestowed on earth, whereas the rewards of believers are to be received in heaven (Matthew 5:12). This time is apparently spoken of in Isaiah 40:10, "Behold, the LORD GOD will come with might, with His arm ruling for Him. Behold, His reward is with Him." Again in Isaiah 62:11, "Say to the daughter of Zion, 'Lo, your salvation comes; behold His reward is with Him.'" In both cases, this promise is to the Jews and the reward is the redemption of and the new character of Israel for they are to be called "holy people, the redeemed by the LORD" (Isaiah 62:12).

This appears to be a summary of the treatment of the Jews, for the church has been raptured and there is no mention of believers, by those events that are triggered by the seventh trumpet as God brings judgment on the earth and establishes His kingdom as Christ returns.

REVELATION 12

Chapters 12 through 14 are again parenthetical. The bowl judgments released by the sounding of the seventh trumpet in 11:15 are not described until chapter 16.

Verses 1-2

Chapter 12 opens with the introduction of a "great sign" that appears in heaven. That it is called a "sign" indicates that this is not a literal vision but is a symbol of an important truth or revelation. This sign was "a woman clothed with the sun, and the moon under her feet, and on her head a crown of twelve stars." She is pregnant and in pain due to being in the process of giving birth. To understand this sign, we need to go back to Genesis 37:9-10. Jacob's son Joseph had a dream in which he saw the sun, moon, and eleven stars bowing down to him. In verse 10, these heavenly bodies are identified as his mother, father, and eleven brothers. Jacob's family (and his twelve sons) was the first generation of Israelites. God renamed Jacob, Israel, and Jacob's sons became the ancestors of Israel's twelve tribes. Therefore, the woman's crown of twelve stars is a sign for the nation of Israel.

Verses 3-6

Next John observed a second sign appearing in heaven: "a great red dragon having seven heads and ten horns, and on his heads were seven diadems. And his tail swept away a third of the stars of heaven, and threw them to earth." This dragon stood before the woman, ready to devour the child when she gave birth.

We don't have to look far for the identification of this dragon; verse 9 calls him, "the serpent of old who is called the devil and Satan." In verse 5 the woman (Israel) gives birth to a male child who will rule the nations with a rod of iron (see also Psalm 2:9). The woman's child was "caught up to God and to His throne."

This child could only be the Lord Jesus who was born of Mary. In this scenario, however, we are getting a glimpse into the spiritual battle that surrounded the birth of Jesus Christ in that stable in Bethlehem. As quiet and peaceful as we might picture that scene, the birth of God's Son started a spiritual battle with Satan that continues to this day. Clearly, Satan hoped to keep the child from being born.

It appears that God is showing to the court of twenty-four elders and to John a summary of His case against Satan revealing cosmic concerns rather than telling the stories of the individual humans who were used to accomplish the results God had predestined. He therefore considers Christ to have been born of the nation of Israel, with no mention of Mary, skips the development of Israel as a nation, and begins His condemnation of Satan with Christ's birth, skips the details of His crucifixion and death and resurrection (possibly because Christ's death was voluntary and not due to Satan's intervention), but emphasizes His ascension to heaven. He then skips the age of grace and moves on over two thousand years to the end time and to the action of the woman (Israel) fleeing into the wilderness to a place prepared by God so she might be nourished for 1,260 days, apparently to avoid further attempts by Satan to destroy her. Some believe that the old Nabathean city of Petra, carved out of sandstone in southern Jordan, may be this place of refuge. It seems to me that wherever the place may be, it will have to be protected supernaturally for with today's technology and Satan's roving demons I don't believe it would be possible to hide several million people from Satan's fury and power anywhere on earth. But, it seems that is just what God is saying in this passage, for He says that the woman will go to "a place prepared by God." Again, the time period for this protection of Israel is 1,260 days (three-and-a-half years), covering the same window of time that the nations will be treading Jerusalem under foot and that the two witnesses will be prophesying.

Returning to the description of Satan, there are two mysteries. The first is the meaning of the seven heads, ten horns, and the diadems. For information on this mystery we must look to Scripture. Each time "heads" and "horns" are mentioned in context similar to this passage (as in Daniel 7 and Revelation 17, for instance), both heads and horns symbolize kings or kingdoms. The appearance of "diadems" on the heads in this passage re-enforces that title, for diadems designate royalty.

So what do the seven heads and ten horns on the dragon signify? Revelation 17:9-12 answers that question: The seven heads are seven mountains (kingdoms) and they are seven kings—five have fallen, one is, the other has not yet come. The ten horns are ten kings who have not yet received a kingdom. This phenomenon of seven heads and ten horns is discussed in more detail in chapters 13 and 17, but for now, suffice it to identify the heads as the six kingdoms that controlled Israel—Egypt, Assyria, Babylon, Medo-Persia, Greece, and Rome. These six kingdoms are those which Satan has controlled over thousands of years during his actions against Israel in his attempts to stop Christ's advent. A possible clue to this control may have been presented in Daniel 10 (which was discussed earlier in Revelation 5), when the angel messenger battled both the prince of Persia and prince of Greece. Both of these princes were demons in Satan's hierarchy and the countries they represented had been involved in the capture and occupation of Israel at various times in history. The seventh head and ten horns refer to the kingdom of the antichrist and the ten kings Satan controls through the antichrist in his last attempt to destroy Israel and rule the world.

The second mystery is the meaning of the stars swept out of heaven to earth. The matter of the stars being thrown to earth was addressed earlier in 9:1-2. As noted there, these stars are fairly certain to be those angels that followed Satan when he was first removed from his most exalted position in Eden, the garden of God, and cast from the mountain of God (Ezekiel 28:11-19), which is probably the time Christ saw Satan fall from heaven (Luke 10:18).

Verses 7-12

The next verses focus on a war that occurs in heaven between Michael and his angels and Satan and his angels. This conflict ends with the defeat of Satan and his being thrown out of heaven with his angels and down to earth where he had already been deceiving the whole world. This action resulted in rejoicing in heaven saying, "Now the salvation, and the power, and the kingdom of our God and the authority of His Christ have come, for the accuser of our brethren has been thrown down, who accuses them before our God day and night. And they overcame him because of the blood of the Lamb and because of the word of their testimony, and they did not love their life even to death." So for this reason, those who dwell in heaven rejoice, but woe to the earth for the devil has come down with great wrath, knowing his time is short.

We know that Satan has had authority on the earth as well as access to heaven since his removal from his post in the garden of God. In John 14:30 as Christ prepared for His coming arrest and death, He said to His disciples that "the ruler of the world is coming," referring to Satan. In Ephesians 2:2 Paul indicated that the Ephesians had been made alive with Christ and saved from the sins in which they formerly walked according to the "prince of the power of the air." First John 5:19 states that "the whole world lies in the power of the evil one." Ephesians 6:12 is even more inclusive as it states, "Our struggle is not against flesh and blood, but against the rulers, against the powers, against the world forces of this darkness, against the spiritual forces of wickedness in the heavenly places." In Luke 22:31 Christ tells Simon Peter that "Satan has demanded permission to sift you like wheat."

Then in several passages we are informed that Satan also was allowed activity in heaven before God. In Job 1, Satan appeared before God along with the sons of God and challenged Job's faithfulness. In Zechariah 3:1, Satan stood before the angel of the Lord to accuse Joshua, which was one of the reasons his removal from heaven was a reason for rejoicing—that is, he was an accuser of the brethren. This is a mystery we don't understand and Scripture gives us no clue as to why Satan was allowed this privilege of continued access to God after his demotion.

It is possible that Satan had been a faithful servant. In Ezekiel 28:12 and 15 Satan is described as having "the seal of perfection, full of wisdom and perfect in beauty" as well as being "blameless in your ways from the day you were created, until unrighteousness was found in you." Satan apparently was one of God's most excellent creations and was held in high esteem by God, for he held one of the highest positions in God's dominion. He may have held this position and had a special relationship to God for thousands of years before he was found to be unrighteous. We just don't know what this relationship may have been, but we do know God is righteous and full of grace. He may have extended this grace to Satan and given him a second chance as He does we humans, but when Satan turned on His Son, as described in Revelation 12, God's anger was aroused and His patience came to an end. Satan was denied any further access to heaven and was thrown to the earth after Michael and his angels defeated Satan in a war in heaven.

This war is similar to the one in Daniel 10, where the messenger fought against the prince of Persia, and as was discussed there, how are these battles between such formidable foes, that are apparently indestructible, conducted? However, as pointed out in verse 11, "and they overcame him (Satan) because of the blood of the Lamb and because of the word of their testimony, and they did not love their life even to death." So in some way those who were martyred in Christ had an influence on Satan's being expelled from heaven, which resulted in rejoicing in heaven, so Satan's presence there must have been the cause of some dysfunction in the heavenly family for thousands of years.

Verses 13-17

Having been finally thrown out of heaven, having failed to stop the arrival of God's Son, and being refused further access to God, Satan realized that he has only a short time (remember that he knows Scripture). In anger he turned his attention to the remaining Jewish nation with the intent of destroying them. Perhaps he thinks that if he can destroy the Jewish nation, he would be able to nullify the various covenants entered into by God with the Jewish nation (through Noah, Abraham, and David). That would at least give Satan a "one up" on God by showing that God did not have enough power to keep His promises Satan would then still be in charge of the earth.

Whatever his reasoning, Satan began to persecute "the woman" (Israel). The woman was given wings that she might fly into a safe place where she would be nourished for a time, and times, and half a time (three-and-a-half years). This is in accord with Christ's admonition to the Jews in Matthew 24:15-16, "Therefore when you see the ABOMI-NATION OF DESOLATION which was spoken of through Daniel the prophet, standing in the holy place (let the reader understand), then let those who are in Judea flee to the mountains." (Note that His concern here is the Jewish nation only as He speaks to those in Judea and not to the rest of the world.)

This time is also referred to in Daniel 12:1 where Daniel was told by the messenger that "Michael, the great prince who stands guard over the sons of your people, will arise. And there will be a time of distress such as never occurred since there was a nation until that time; and at that time your people, everyone who is found in the book, will be rescued." This prophecy apparently is fulfilled as the woman is removed to a place of safety, probably by Michael who just completed the battle with Satan in heaven. The woman is Israel, but apparently not all the Jews will be transported to safety; Daniel indicates that only those recorded in the book will be saved. Who and how many there will be we are not told in either passage. However, we may get a clue from Zechariah 13:8-9 which is thought to refer to this time. Zechariah wrote that two-thirds of the people will be cut off, and the third part will be brought through the fire and be refined. It is also unclear which "book" Daniel was referring to, but it evidently relates to the Jewish people and may be the one Daniel was instructed to close (Daniel 12:4). I believe it may be the same book that is in Christ's hand as He displays the last days of Jewish history to John (Revelation 5:7; 6:1).

Satan then creates a flood to destroy those who have been moved to safety, so he apparently knew where they were. The earth opens up to absorb the flood and protect the people. Those saved must have God's protection, for Satan does not pursue them. Enraged by the failure of his flood, he goes off "to make war with the rest of her offspring, who keep the commandments of God and hold to the testimony of Jesus."

Who these "offspring" are is a matter of speculation. We know from the text that they must be Christians, for they hold to the testimony of Jesus. We also know they are not included with those found in the book and taken to a place of refuge. The fact that they keep the commandments of God has a Jewish connotation. So they may be either Jews or Gentiles who have been saved during the tribulation. Since Satan's primary focus is the Jewish nation, they are probably Jewish Christians who are in Jerusalem and have had exposure to and followed the teaching and prophecy of the two witnesses.

THE BEASTS OF PROPHECY

As chapter 13 opens, John was immediately introduced to a beast coming out of the sea. Some of the most dramatic and misunderstood subjects of prophecy are the various references to beasts in Daniel and Revelation. As we learned in the consideration of Nebuchadnezzar's vision of the great statue (Daniel 2), followed by Daniel's vision of the four beasts (Daniel 7), God and man do not see history in the same way. Nebuchadnezzar saw the great powers as parts of a great image; God saw these same powers as beasts. It is these beasts that we need to consider and how they relate to one another as they arise in Revelation. Each of the beasts has a part in the time of the Gentiles and their control of Israel and is described by the characteristics of its leader, its power, and its style of conquest.

Biblical Reference	Description of the Beast	Identity of the Beast
Daniel 7:4	The first (of four beasts) was like a lion and had the wings of an eagle.	Babylon and Nebuchadne-zzar
Daniel 7:5	A second one, resembling a bear.	Medo-Persia
Daniel 7:6	Another one, like a leopard, which had on its back four wings of a bird; the beast also had four heads and dominion was given to it.	Greece and Alexander

Daniel 7:7	A fourth beast, dreadful and terrifying and extremely strong; had large iron teeth. It devoured, crushed, and trampled the remainder (the Jews) with its feet; it was different than all the beasts that were before it; it had ten horns.	The antichrist
Revelation 11:7	This verse references the beast that comes out of the abyss, which is described further in Revelation 17:8, who makes war with the two witnesses and kills them	The antichrist
Revelation 13:1	This beast is described as coming up out of the sea and having seven heads and ten horns with diadems on the horns and blasphemous names on the heads	The antichrist
13:2	It was like a leopard with feet like a bear and a mouth like a lion. The dragon of chapter 12 (Satan) gave the beast his power, his throne, and great authority.	
13:3	One of the heads appeared to have been slain and the wound healed.	
13:5	He spoke arrogant words and blasphemies against God and was given forty-two months to act.	
13:7	It was also given to him to make war with the saints and overcome them, and to have authority over every tribe and nation. All will worship him.	

Revelation 13:11	Another beast appears arising from the earth, and he had two horns like a lamb and spoke like a dragon. He exercises all the authority of the first beast, but only when in his presence. He makes all who dwell on the earth worship the first beast whose fatal wound was healed (note that this was one of seven heads in the description of the first beast). He performs great signs and deceives the people. He tells them to worship an image of the beast (probably set up in the temple, 2 Thessalonians 2:4), under penalty of death for failure to do so. His final act is to set up the mark of the beast as a requirement to buy or sell.	The false prophet
Revelation 17:3 17:8 17:11 17:16-17	A woman was sitting on this beast which was scarlet and had seven heads and ten horns and was full of blasphemous names. This beast was, is not, and is about to come up out of the abyss. This beast is an eighth and is one of the seven and goes to destruction. The beast will hate the harlot along with the ten horns, and the horns will give their kingdoms to the beast to fulfill God's purpose of destroying the harlot.	The antichrist
Revelation 19:19-20	The beast and the kings of the earth are prepared to make war against Christ. The beast and false prophet who performed the signs in his presence and deceived those who received the mark of the beast were both seized and thrown into the lake of fire.	The antichrist and the false prophet

Five beasts are described in Daniel and Revelation—they are Babylon, Medo-Persia, Greece, the antichrist, and the false prophet. The first three are mentioned and identified only in Daniel as part of Daniel's visions of the full scope of the time of the Gentiles. Babylon is the first beast in chapter 7 as Daniel had a vision of four beasts. Medo-Persia and Greece were identified in chapter 8 in Daniel's ram and goat vision, and were the second and third beasts in chapter 7. The fourth beast (or antichrist) is introduced in Daniel 7:7, and further described in Revelation 13 and 17. He is not identified specifically as the antichrist in either instance. In each case, his description includes a reference to ten horns as well as other extreme characteristics—such as crushing and trampling the remainder or making war with the saints and overcoming them, both phrases referring to the Jews and his attempt to destroy them; these descriptions identify the beast as the antichrist. The false prophet is introduced in Revelation 13:11 and is specifically identified in 19:20. More commentary regarding the beasts will be found in Revelation chapters 13, 17, and 19.

REVELATION 13

Verses 1-2

"And he stood on the sand of the seashore." The opening sentence of chapter 13 leaves us uncertain as to who is standing on the seashore. Some believe it was John and replace "he" with "I." Some treat this verse as the last sentence of chapter 12, in which case it would be the dragon, Satan, who is standing on the seashore. The NASB changed its translation from "And he" in earlier editions to "And the dragon" in more recent editions, indicating that the translators considered "he" to be Satan. Whoever it may be, the next sentence makes it clear that John saw a beast coming up out of the sea.

As we discussed in the section on the antichrist in the commentary following Revelation 5, when "sea" is used in Scripture in a generic sense, it usually refers to Gentile humanity (as in Daniel 7:2-8; and Matthew 13:47-49). This beast arising from the sea (Gentile community) is defined by its looks—John describes it as having ten horns with diadems on each, and seven heads on which were blasphemous names. It was like a leopard, but with feet like those of a bear and a mouth like that of a lion. The dragon, who was described as Satan in chapter 12, proceeds to give this beast his power, great authority, and even his throne.

We are helped in understanding this beast by returning to Daniel 7 where Daniel saw several beasts with characteristics similar to those seen by John. The leopard was Alexander the Great of Macedonia or Greece, the bear was Medo-Persia, and the lion Nebuchadnezzar or Babylon. Each of the beasts in Daniel's vision represented kingdoms. In Daniel, the use of beasts as a descriptive phrase was how God sees these kingdoms, not as man would see them. In God's view, all satanically controlled humans or human organizations are no more than beasts. As Solomon noted in Ecclesiastes 3:18-22, the man under the sun (natural man) is as mortal as any beast if he does not become aware of what will come after him (eternity). And in Psalm 49:20 David wrote, "Man in his pomp, yet without understanding, is like the beasts that perish."

According to John's observation, the beast coming out of the sea either has the characteristics of three of Daniel's four beasts (leopard, lion, and bear) or it is made up of the nations that are a modern equivalent of three of Daniel's four beasts. I believe it is probably the latter. A composite of those nations that are the modern equivalent of those three beasts of Daniel make up the beast that John saw coming out of the sea. A comparison of the biblical maps outlining the Babylonian, Medo-Persian, and Grecian empires (the general boundaries of all three of these historic kingdoms roughly circumscribe the same land area) with today's atlas of national boundaries indicates that the following countries could be included in the fourth beast's kingdom: Pakistan, Afghanistan, Kyrgystan, Tajikstan, Uzbekistan, Turkmenistan (these last four were part of Russia until recently), Iran, Iraq, Syria, Turkey, Jordan, Egypt, and Greece, and possibly Libya, Armenia, Georgia, and Azerbaijan. Some or all of these may be the beast spoken of by John, however, ultimately there will be ten of these nations that are brought under the influence and control of the antichrist.

The fourth beast in Daniel 7 was, apparently, the same beast that John saw here and it is described in more detail in Daniel as the vision is interpreted in Daniel 7:19-25. In verses 7 and 19, this beast is said to be dreadful, extremely strong, with large iron teeth and claws of bronze It is also said to devour, crush, and trample the remainder (that is, the wearing down of the saints spoken of in verse 25). Clearly, this beast is different from all the other beasts. Additional details are mentioned in verse 23 where the fourth beast is said to be a fourth kingdom that will be different from all the other kingdoms; it will devour the whole earth. In verse 24, the ten horns are discussed. They are ten kings that arise out of this beast or kingdom, and another horn will arise after them and subdue three of the kings. This horn who is not described as a king will speak against the Most High and wear down His saints. He will intend to change time and the law, and he will have time, times, and half time (three-and-a-half years) to do all of this. The beast seen by John coming out of the sea (Gentile humanity) (Revelation 13:1) and Daniel's fourth beast (and little horn that arises out of it) are two representations of the antichrist.

The head and horn characteristics have been prominent in three other places. First, in Daniel, the fourth and final beast was described as having ten horns (Daniel 7:7). Second, in Revelation 12:3, the dragon was described as having seven heads and ten horns with diadems on the heads. Then finally, in Revelation 17:3, John is shown a woman sitting on a scarlet beast; this beast also has seven heads and ten horns, and it is full of blasphemous names. In Revelation 17:9-12, the seven heads are described as seven mountains and seven kings, and the ten horns are described as ten kings who have not received a kingdom, but they receive authority as kings with the beast for one hour.

Based upon Revelation 17:9-12 (discussed in the commentary on chapter 12), each time the seven heads are mentioned, including here in chapter 13, four of them represent the kings or kingdoms that made up four of the beasts seen by Daniel. These were Babylon, Medo-Persia, Greece, and Rome. Two of the seven are those who controlled Israel before Daniel. These were Egypt (Israel's captivity under Pharaoh) and Assyria (under Sennacherib, when the northern kingdom was exiled). The seventh is the antichrist seen by Daniel as the fourth beast and the little horn (Daniel 7:7-8) and by John as the head that was healed. These seven heads mounted on the final beast would appear to imply that they are part of that beast and are still alive.

As the beast coming out of the sea is introduced in Revelation 13:1, the first reaction is that he has the same seven heads and ten horns as did the dragon in 12:3. However, there is a minor difference: in 13:1, the diadems are on the horns; in 12:3, the diadems are on the heads.

The significance of these variances in observation may be in 13:1. The horns with the diadems are shown on the beast coming out of the sea to reflect the ten kings arising from the last beast (antichrist), whereas in 12:3 Satan (the dragon) had diadems on the seven heads which were kingdoms he controlled in his battle to prevent the birth, death, and return of Christ. Whatever the significance of the observations, the heads and the horns signify the same kingdoms and kings in both cases and, of course, wherever Satan is there also is the spirit of the antichrist.

"And the dragon gave him his power and his throne and great authority." This reminds us of the kingdoms of the world and their glory that Satan offered Christ in Matthew 4:8-9 if He would fall down and worship him. It was not an idle offer, for Satan has the authority to grant such power. As we know, Christ did not challenge the credibility of Satan's offer, but He did challenge Satan's claim to be worthy of worship. Christ admonished Satan, saying, "Begone Satan! For it is written, 'YOU SHALL WORSHIP THE LORD YOUR GOD AND SERVE HIM ONLY.'" Here in Revelation, Satan has found his "messiah" and proceeds to anoint the beast to do his work and to give the beast the tools to work with—power, throne, and authority. Apparently Satan has established his throne in this kingdom, for his throne is one of the assets given to the beast. In Daniel 7:23, this beast was said to be different than all of the other beasts: "The fourth beast will be a fourth kingdom on the earth, which will be different from all the other kingdoms." This difference was probably due to the power of Satan given to this last beast.

It appears that this last beast is a revival of all of the nations that have oppressed Israel since their origination, for each of them is represented by one of the seven heads on this final beast. This conforms to Nebuchadnezzar's vision in Daniel 2:31 of the "single great statue" of awesome appearance, as well as its final destruction. The statue's figure represented several nations (the same nations as the beasts, except for Egypt and Assyria), and it was the seamless figure of a man until the "stone was cut out without hands," struck the feet of the statue, and crushed the iron, the bronze, the clay, the silver and the gold in one stroke. So the statue was not destroyed piecemeal, but with one blow by the rock.

Verses 3-6

John next saw one of the seven heads as if it had been slain, but the fatal wound healed. "And the whole earth was amazed and followed after the beast; and they worshiped the dragon, because he gave his authority to the beast; and they worshiped the beast, saying, 'Who is like the beast, and who is able to wage war with him?'"

It appears that, although this beast has seven heads, it is controlled by the head that seems to have been slain but has been healed. There have been many different opinions as to who the "beast" is and how he will return to life after being fatally wounded. Many students of Revelation believe that this person is an historical character such as Antiochus Epiphanes, or someone known to have a head wound, such as John Kennedy. But verse 14 indicates that it was a sword wound. Those who believe that it refers to a person from the past have another hurdle to get over, and that is whether Satan has the power to create or restore life. Most think not. Others do not believe it was a person, but possibly one of the seven kingdoms that had been destroyed, such as Babylon, that will regain its power, and in effect come back to life. None of these possibilities would capture the imagination of the world as described in this passage as would the resurrection of a man who had been effective on the world stage and was well known by all nations.

Referring again to Daniel, the activity of the antichrist is outlined beginning in 11:36. The activity includes blasphemy against God, magnification of himself, taking action against the strongest of fortresses, and war with the kings of the South and North as well as other countries. Then in verse 45 it states that in Israel (called the beautiful Holy Mountain), "he will come to his end, and no one will help him." Then, Daniel 12:1 refers to a "time of distress such as never occurred since there was a nation." The structure of these events seems to indicate that the antichrist faces his end in Jerusalem, presumably his death, after which the great tribulation (the final three-and-a-half years) occurs. Revelation 13 seems to answer the puzzle of how the tribulation could intensify after the antichrist is killed. Verse 13 refers to the head that appeared to have been slain and his fatal wound was healed. Apparently the antichrist is revived after which he is also given great authority by Satan. The passage does speak to the circumstances of his death in that the people asked,

"Who is able to wage war with him?" Apparently his "resurrection" came after a fatal wound during war, so the logical question becomes: If you can't kill him, how can you wage war against him?

After the antichrist is killed in one of the battles mentioned in the Daniel passage near the end of the first three-and-a-half years of the tribulation period, his body could very possibly be possessed by one of Satan's demons. As we have seen in other scriptures, demon possession is not uncommon and can cause the possessed person to perform unusual feats of strength as well as other unusual activities. The world would recognize him as the one who had solved the "Jewish problem" (the covenant mentioned in Daniel 9:27) during his first three-and-a-half years and had been killed in battle. They will, of course, be amazed at his resurrection and respect will turn to worship.

The people worshiped the dragon (Satan) because he had given his authority to the beast and they worshiped the beast. It's interesting that the people would somehow know that Satan had given his authority to the beast and so, in their eyes, he deserved to be worshiped. Satan is the great counterfeiter or deceiver (2 Thessalonians 2:8-10) and he would have the antichrist mimic Christ's comment in John 14:9, "He who has seen Me has seen the Father." Satan would certainly want to be worshiped, so in some way he lets the world know that it was his power flowing from the antichrist.

Chapter 13 opens as Satan observes the beast (antichrist) arising from the Gentile population and prepares him for the final three-and-a-half years of the tribulation. As was indicated earlier, initially the antichrist is very likely to be a well-respected person from the Arab states due to his success during his first three-and-a-half years in developing a treaty or covenant with the Jews that is acceptable to the Arab and Palestinian people. There will be wars and conflict during his first three-and-a-half years, but he may be rather moderate and forbearing during this time compared to the atrocities of his last three-and-a-half years when he has the power of Satan. Although the time of this scene of the beast coming out of the sea is not mentioned, it does appear that it is after he has been killed in war and is then revived at the beginning of the last three-and-a-half years of his reign.

The vision then moves to the transfer of power and throne by Satan to the antichrist and almost simultaneously John observes one of the heads as if it had been slain and his fatal wound healed. It is after the fatal head wound is healed that the antichrist begins speaking out, empowered by Satan, with arrogant words that blaspheme God and His tabernacle—that is, those who dwell in heaven. This conforms to the comments in Daniel 11:36, that this king will "speak monstrous things against the God of gods." It appears that blasphemy is not an incidental feature of Satan's kingdom but one of the main features. This may be another reason Satan was thrown out of heaven. It seems that, up until this time, his purpose had been to accuse the saints; at this time he will demean God and those who dwell in heaven.

The final comment in verse 5 is that he is given authority to act for forty-two months, which corresponds to three-and-a-half years. The consistency of the use of that length of time to depict the final period of the antichrist's reign leads to the conclusion that whenever the forty-two months are mentioned, they refer to the last three-and-a-half years of the tribulation, referred to as the great tribulation by Christ in Matthew 24:21. Since these months are granted to the beast or antichrist subsequent to his death and seeming resurrection, the logical conclusion is that, to fulfill the prophecy of a seven year reign in Daniel 9:27, he must have reigned three-and-a-half years prior to his death.

Verse 7

The antichrist's power is extended as "it was also given to him to make war with the saints and to overcome them, and authority over every tribe and people and tongue and nation was given him." Some believe these abilities were given to the antichrist by Satan, which I'm sure is true, but it seems that it was also due to the removal of the restraining influence of the "restrainer" (Holy Spirit) mentioned in 2 Thessalonians 2:6-7. This, then, is the beginning of the specific persecution of Jews and those who become believers in Christ during these terrible times. It was also during this same period of time (three-and-a-half years) that the Lord will give authority to His two witnesses to prophesy, described in chapter 11, who will ultimately be killed by the beast that comes out of the abyss (11:7), or antichrist, as part of his war against the saints.

Verse 7 indicates that the antichrist will have authority over every tribe, tongue, and nation—all will worship him. The term "authority over" is not defined, but depending on the size and discipline of his organization, it could be quite oppressive or it could be loose and disorganized. I would suspect that his organization would be quite disciplined and oppressive in the Middle East, but quite loose, if even applicable, in the rest of the world.

Verses 8-10

It is re-emphasized that anyone who dwells on earth, whose name had not been written in the Lamb's book of life from the foundation of the world, will worship the beast (antichrist). Then comes the warning that was used frequently in the first three chapters of Revelation, "If anyone has an ear, let him hear." In this case, however, the familiar phrase, "what the Spirit says to the churches" is missing. This could be due to the fact that the church has been raptured, but also may be because the Lord is speaking to the Jews whose ears have been closed for centuries by His judgment in Isaiah 6, which was discussed in the commentary on Revelation 2:7.

Verse 10 seems to be speaking to the saints with whom the antichrist makes war, that some are destined for captivity and others will be killed. These persecutions will test their faith and perseverance.

Verses 11-15

John next sees another beast coming up out of the earth. This beast has "two horns like a lamb and he spoke as a dragon." Most students of Revelation believe that the reference to "sea" regarding the first beast indicates that it will come from the Gentile population. Many believe that reference to the "earth" here indicates that this second beast will come from the Jewish nation. There does not seem to be indication of this in the text. It does seem, however, that he may be a religious leader due to his appearance as a lamb and his religious activities relating to the beast. He may possibly be the head of the apostate church that is prominent after the rapture of the true church. He speaks, however, like a dragon, and the only dragon we know of is identified as Satan. He exercises all the authority of the first beast when he is in the presence of the first beast, whose fatal wound was healed. There is no indication as to why he has authority only in the presence of the first beast. Possibly there is no love or trust lost between them. In 16:13, this second beast is called the "false prophet" and his arrival on the scene completes the evil trinity.

The second beast or false prophet makes those who dwell on the earth worship the first beast (antichrist), telling them to create an image of the first beast to which image he is able to give breath, so that the image can speak. Some have questioned the ability of the image to speak, implying that it is through some contrivance such as radio, robot, or ventriloquism. Considering the sophistication of today's audience, such obvious contrivances would not fool very many. It is probably a real power, for verse 15 says, "There was given to him to give breath to the image of the beast, that the image of the beast might even speak." There is no indication as to who gives him this power. I suppose that the ability of the image to breathe and speak could be only the indwelling of a demon in the image; however, the passage does say that the second beast (false prophet) gave breath to the image. The false prophet is also able to perform great signs in the presence of the first beast, deceiving those who dwell on earth.

There is no indication in this passage as to the location of this image; however, Christ said in Matthew 24:15 that it would be in "the holy place," and Paul wrote in 2 Thessalonians 2:4 that the man of lawlessness would take "his seat in the temple of God." The image must, therefore, be in Jerusalem and the order to worship the image of the beast or be killed is probably applicable to the Jewish population.

Verses 16-18

The beast establishes the infamous "mark of the beast" (13:16). No one can buy or sell without the name of the beast or the number of his name, 666, on his right hand or forehead. There has been much speculation about the number 666; however, Scripture gives no explanation except to imply that if we have wisdom, we should be able to calculate the number of beast. The most popular thought is that, since the number 7 indicates perfection, then the number of the Father, Son, and Holy

Spirit would be 777. Comparatively the number of Satan, the antichrist, and the false prophet would fall far short of perfection represented by the lesser numbers for each of the evil trinity: 666.

This false prophet seems to be a fulfillment of the last part of Daniel 9:27, "On the wing of abominations will come one who makes desolate." Christ referred to this time in Matthew 24:15-16, "Therefore when you see the ABOMINATION OF DESOLATION which was spoken of through Daniel the prophet, standing in the holy place (let the reader understand), then let those who are in Judea flee to the mountains."

It is obvious that the activities of both the antichrist and the false prophet are focused in Israel as evidenced by Christ addressing His remark to those "in Judea." In addition, there are several other matters which imply that the focus of the evil forces will be on Israel. The image of the beast will be mounted in the temple in Jerusalem, according to Matthew 24:15 and 2 Thessalonians 2:4. The antichrist and the false prophet will be preoccupied by the two witnesses who are conducting their activities in Jerusalem. The "mark of the beast" (Revelation 13:16) is initiated immediately after the image is installed (13:15) in the temple, indicating that the "mark" may be instituted only in Israel. The "mark" may even be Satan's response to and imitation of God's sealing of the 144,000, which applied only to the Jews (Revelation 7:4). I believe that due to time constraints (three-and-a-half years) and Satan's focus on the Jewish people, the antichrist will have little influence on the day-to-day affairs of the rest of the world. The world's worship of him will probably be rather limited from afar, similar to the public adoration often given to public figures.

REVELATION 14

Verses 1-5

After seeing the second beast from the earth in chapter 13, John's next view is of Christ (the Lamb) standing on Mount Zion with the 144,000 who apparently are those sealed as bond-servants of God in 7:3-8. The text is not clear as to whether this scene is on earth or in heaven, for Mount Zion is used to describe both the earthly and heavenly Jerusalem.

Many believe that the scene is on earth The four angels who had an assignment to effect the earth were told to stop until the sealing of the 144,000 had taken place (7:3). This pause gave the impression that these were to be sealed to protect them from the judgments during the tribulation. Other than being exempt from the sting of the locusts in 9:4, there is no indication of the purpose of their sealing. Those exempt had the seal of God on their foreheads, and were presumably this group. Many consider the 144,000 to be missionaries on earth, after having been sealed as servants of God, and having a significant role in the conversion of many who were in the great multitude in chapter 7. There is, however, no indication in Scripture that they are sealed for the purpose of being missionaries.

There are several reasons to consider the scene to be in heaven. In Hebrews 12:22 and 24, Paul, speaking to Christians comparing the old covenant and the fearful presence of God to the new covenant in Jesus, stated very clearly that "you have come to Mount Zion and to the city of the living God, the heavenly Jerusalem…and to Jesus." Paul then issued a warning about turning away from Him who warned from heaven (Hebrews 12:25). Paul, therefore, tied Christ and his location to the heavenly Mount Zion. Second, Christ is in the process of performing His role as judge, and that role is exercised from heaven. Third, there is no indication that Christ comes to earth prior to His glorious second coming. If He were on the earthly Mount Zion, it would have to be after His second advent; there is no indication that is what occurred. In Revelation 11:15-19, the kingdom of the world is declared to have become the kingdom of Christ; He has taken God's great power and has begun to reign. Verse 19 indicates the temple of God, which is in heaven, is opened and the ark of His covenant appears in His temple. This is probably where Christ is as He stands on Mount Zion in chapter 14, having been given the earthly kingdom but not yet descended with His great army to wage war and rule the nations (as is described in chapter 19). He is standing with the very select 144,000 Jewish men who were sealed by having "His name and the name of His Father written on their foreheads" (14:1).

The men have several distinct characteristics. They are all Jewish. They are sealed quite differently than are we, the members of the church, who are sealed by the indwelling of the Holy Spirit. These men have been selected because they had not been defiled with women, having kept themselves chaste. Some believe this is a symbolic description indicating they had nothing to do with the pagan system of worship; however, that they kept themselves "chaste" certainly has a sexual connotation. There is no lie found in them, and they are blameless. It is probably in the context of Romans 1:17-32 (where Paul described ungodliness and unrighteousness) that the 144,000 are considered blameless. In 1:25 Paul stated that such ungodly people "exchanged the glory of the incorruptible God for an image in the form of corruptible man and of birds and four-footed animals and crawling creatures." Then in verses 26-32, Paul delineated the depraved condition of the ungodly, including sexual immorality and even homosexuality.

Twice the text mentions that the 144,000 were "purchased" from the earth. I presume that means through the blood of Christ, as was the church. They do, however, have three additional distinct characteristics. First, they sing a new song (verse 3). Since no one else can learn the song, it has to be the 144,000 singing, and they sing it before the throne and the four living creatures and the elders. This, again, places them in heaven. Second, they follow the Lamb wherever He goes. Third, they are first fruits to God and to the Lamb. The text does not explain what each of these characteristics means. There has been considerable speculation in that regard, so a few more thoughts may not clarify nor will they confuse the issue any more than it is already. God obviously inserted this scene and verbal commentary from the voice in heaven for some purpose or to express some truth. It seems that this may have a relationship to the truth expressed in Romans 11:5 where Paul indicated that there was a remnant in Elijah's day, and there is, also, a remnant in Paul's day, who had not succumbed to the widespread apostasy and had remained faithful according to God's gracious choice. The other Jews, who had not been chosen, were hardened under the judgment given to Isaiah to exercise (Isaiah 6:9), so they could not understand God's grace (Romans 11:6-10). God took this opportunity to graft the Gentiles into the "root" in place of those Jewish "branches" that had been broken off, so Israel's loss was riches for the Gentiles (Romans 11:12). There will come a day, however, when the fullness of the Gentiles has come in and all Israel will be saved (Romans 11:25-26). As Paul expressed in 11:15, "For if their [the Jews] rejection be the reconciliation of the world, what will their acceptance be but life from the dead?" Then he follows that up in verse 16, "And if the first piece of dough be holy, the lump is also; and if the root be holy, the branches are too."

So, let's go back to applying this truth to the passage in Revelation. The time of the Gentiles is ended with the declaration that the kingdom of the world has become the kingdom of our Lord and His Christ (Revelation 11:15). It is, therefore, time for opening the eyes and the understanding of the Jews. There is a chosen remnant of 144,000 who had not succumbed to the apostasy after the rapture of the church, and these become that holy first fruit or "first piece of dough" to enter the kingdom and pave the way for Israel to finally understand and accept the

Messiah. It could well be that the song (that only they could learn, for only the Jews could sing it) was to ask for the return of their Messiah in accord with Christ's statement in Matthew 23:39 as He agonized over Jerusalem, "For I say to you, from now on you shall not see Me until you say 'BLESSED IS HE WHO COMES IN THE NAME OF THE LORD!'"

Verses 6-8

John sees another angel flying in midheaven having an eternal gospel to preach to those on earth, and he does so in a loud voice. "Fear God, and give Him glory, because the hour of His judgment has come; and worship Him who made the heaven and the earth and sea and springs of waters." This is not the gospel of grace with which we are familiar, for to be effective that gospel must be administered by the Holy Spirit—and He has been removed from the earth. It is, as it says, the eternal gospel, which has been from the beginning, consisting of God's glory, His creation of the heaven and the earth, and His judgments. The everlasting good news is that the hour of His judgment has come and that God is about to deal with the earth in righteousness and establish His kingdom.

It could be said that for those who had not accepted the gospel of grace, this is the only gospel they will have—that is, to worship God. The emphasis of this angel's message is God's glory and His creation. This may well be because Satan has so convinced the world that God did not create anything and that He is probably nonexistent, so the truth must begin back at the beginning. Satan's process of deception may have already begun as our educational system and courts struggle to maintain Darwinian evolution as the only creative system to be taught in our schools. This may be the major blasphemy of Satan. In Matthew 24:14, Christ said, "This gospel of the kingdom shall be preached in the whole world for a witness to all the nations, and then the end shall come." Many expositors interpret this to mean the gospel of grace and that may be correct, but it seems that it is most likely referring to the eternal gospel preached to the whole world by this angel.

A second angel is next on the scene, announcing the fall of Babylon the great, "she who has made all the nations drink of the wine of the passion of her immorality." This announcement may be in anticipation of the actual destruction of Babylon as described in chapters 17 and

18, or, since this announcement comes right after the angel with the eternal gospel, it may be the announcement that Babylon, and those who participated in her immorality, had fallen from God's grace and were to be judged.

Verses 9-13

A third angel appears, following the first two, with a warning which he announces with a loud voice, "If anyone worships the beast and his image, and receives a mark on his forehead or upon his hand, he also will drink of the wine of the wrath of God, which is mixed in full strength in the cup of His anger; and he will be tormented with fire and brimstone in the presence of the holy angels and in the presence of the Lamb." The angel goes on to say that these people who worship the beast and receive his mark will be tormented and will have no rest day or night forever.

Following these scenes of warning and judgment, John hears a voice in heaven with an announcement of encouragement to saints who persevere in keeping the commandments of God and their faith in Jesus, "Blessed are the dead who die in the Lord from now on!" This is the second beatitude (blessing) in Revelation. These will die because of their faith and refusal to worship the beast or its image or receive his mark. The Holy Spirit completes the comment, confirming the blessing expressed by the voice from heaven, by saying, "Yes…that they may rest from their labors, for their deeds follow with them." Apparently the Holy Spirit, who is so active in our regeneration and salvation, has a role to play in the salvation of those who are saved after the rapture of the church. His comment is made from heaven, an indication that He is there after the rapture and no longer on earth. His would no longer be an indwelling service, as with us, but it does appear that He has some confirming and possibly "sealing" role to accomplish, which may be necessary in conjunction with Christ's role in verses 14-16.

Verse 14-20

The remainder of the chapter deals with one like a son of man, with a golden crown on His head. He has a sickle in His hand and is told by an angel coming out of the temple to reap the earth for the harvest is ripe. It does not say what is ripe or what is reaped. This appears to be Jesus, but He is told to reap by an angel. It would be unusual for Jesus to be instructed by an angel, however, this particular angel comes out of the temple, and presumably from the presence of the Father, so he could be delivering the Father's message. The translators consider it to be Jesus for they present "He" in the upper case.

Another angel comes out of the temple with a sickle, followed by the angel who has power over fire. The second angel tells the first angel to gather the clusters from the vines of the earth, for her grapes are ripe. The first does as he is told and thrusts his sickle to the earth; those he gathers he throws into the great wine press of the wrath of God. So, in the latter case we are told the reaping is of grapes and then we conclude that this is only symbolic of people, for it is blood that flows from God's wine press not the juice of grapes.

The actions of the two reapers appear to be different. The first one (verse 14) is Christ, and His reaping will be of those who have been saved during the tribulation. This is indicated by 14:13 regarding the Holy Spirit's blessing on those who die "from now on," keeping their faith in Jesus. That these are Christians being reaped does raise the question of how these faithful are "reaped"? It may be that the death of a believer after the rapture would no longer result in being present with the Lord when one is absent from the body (see 1 Corinthians 5:3). This may be the reason for the Spirit's comment in Revelation 14:13. He had to confirm these martyred believers before they could be reaped; otherwise, I can see no reason for the statement in verse 13. These reaped here may well be the multitude in chapter 7 that came out of the great tribulation.

The second reaper is an angel, and it is clear that he reaps those who are destined for the wrath of God. The last verse indicates how terrible that wrath will be—the blood that comes out of the wine press reaches to the horses' bridles for a distance of two hundred miles. This does not seem possible, but someone has made a calculation that if the army spoken of in 9:16 (two-hundred-million men plus their horses) was annihilated, their blood would be about four feet deep, or to a horse's bridle, for about two hundred miles. As noted in chapter 9, I believe that the two hundred million refers to an army of demons, not men, but if this hypothetical calculation is correct, it gives some idea as to how great the angel's killing field will be to result in that much blood. The angel will probably not be the killing instrument but will make it happen in some way, so we look for events that appear to result in significant amounts of bloodshed.

This event has all of the characteristics of the scenario described in Joel 3 in which the Lord gathers all the nations, brings them down to the valley of Jehoshaphat, and enters into judgment with them there. Joel 3:13-14 describes a killing field much like the one above. The Lord says, "Put in the sickle, for the harvest is ripe. Come, tread, for the wine press is full; the vats overflow, for their wickedness is great. Multitudes, multitudes in the valley of decision! For the day of the LORD is near in the valley of decision." The valley of Jehoshaphat has been thought to be the Kidron valley that runs between Jerusalem and the Mount of Olives.

The gathering of nations is similar to that scene we will see in Revelation 16:14-16, in which demons, performing signs, will draw the kings of the whole world together in a place called Armageddon for the war of the great day of God, the Almighty. This battle is, I believe, first described in Isaiah 63:3, and then further in Joel 3, and finally in Revelation 19:15. In all of these scriptures there is reference to the tremendous shedding of blood in the wine press of God's wrath. It appears they all refer to the same judgment, which would be the battle known as Armageddon.

REVELATION 15

Verse 1

As the parenthetical chapters 12–14 come to a close, we move into the next chapter where John sees another great and marvelous sign in heaven: seven angels who have seven plagues. These are the last plagues, for in them the wrath of God is finished. John indicates that the appearance of the angels is "another" sign, thereby including this scene on the same level as the other two signs which were disclosed in chapter 12—one was the woman with child, identified as the nation of Israel; the other was the red dragon, identified as Satan. That this scene is described as a "sign" indicates that it is a symbol of something that may be different than what it appears to be. In this case, however, it quickly becomes a reality as in verses 6 and 7, John sees the seven angels come out of the temple, and each is given a golden bowl full of the wrath of God. Therefore, the first scene, the "great and marvelous" sign, must have some other implication.

We can only speculate as to what that may be. Some commentators think that the three signs are related and are a summary of the prophetic scene of Israel (the woman), Satan and his control of the world, and God's final judgment of Satan and his world system. Picking up on this theme, it appears that if the three "signs" are related, it is more likely they are focused on Christ—the first being His birth and rejection by

Israel, the second being the intent and effort of Satan to destroy Him, and the third being God's ultimate judgment on Israel, the world, and Satan for their rejection of His Son.

Verses 2-4

After seeing the sign, John sees those who were victorious over the beast and his image standing on something like a sea of glass mixed with fire. Apparently these are the people who were martyred for refusing to have the mark of the beast placed in their hand or forehead and refusing to worship his image. They are singing two songs, one being the song of Moses and the other the song of the Lamb. The song of Moses is undoubtedly sung by the Jewish contingent who had been obedient to the word, while the song of the Lamb is sung by those who had been steadfast to their faith in Christ.

There are two instances in the Old Testament where Moses sang his message to the Lord. The first is in Exodus 15 where he and the people of Israel sang a song of praise to the Lord extolling Him for His destruction of Pharaoh's army and protecting Israel in its flight from Egypt. Moses' second song is in Deuteronomy 32 and is quite different from the first. In this song, he ascribes greatness to God and extols His just ways, His perfection, His faithfulness, and His righteousness. Moses then set forth at some length a description of Israel's unfaithfulness and perverseness, how the people forsook the God who made them and scorned the Rock of their salvation. He described how God will heap misfortune on them for these failures. But in Deuteronomy 32:41-43, God was also described as taking vengeance on His people's adversaries. Since the people described here in heaven are singing one of Moses' songs, it was probably the one from Deuteronomy 32. It would be sung as a reminder to Israel of its unfaithfulness to God since the days of Moses—and that is the reason for the judgments that have fallen and are about to fall on that nation.

Unlike the case of Moses' song, there is no "song of the Lamb" identified elsewhere in Scripture. It could very well be the song that was sung at the time Christ took the book in chapter 5. The quotation of the song here in Revelation 15 indicates that both songs close with saying, "Great and marvelous are Thy works, O Lord God, the Almighty;

righteous and true are Thy ways, Thou King of the nations. Who will not fear, O Lord, and glorify Thy name? For Thou alone art holy; for ALL THE NATIONS WILL COME AND WORSHIP BEFORE THEE, for Thy righteous acts have been revealed."

The last time there was reference to the sea of glass was in chapter 4. It was before the throne with only the twenty-four elders seated on thrones and the four living creatures visible. The sea of glass is visible in this scene, but there is no reference to the throne and the victorious group has replaced the twenty-four elders and the four living creatures. Referring back to Daniel 7:21-26, the horn (antichrist) was waging war with the saints and presumably killing many of them until the Ancient of Days came and judgment was passed. Assuming that what John is seeing here is a continuation of Daniel's vision, it appears that the court has completed its work, passed judgment, and has adjourned. The evidence has been presented by the souls of those martyred who are still standing on the sea, and they have provided their testimony before the throne in the songs they sang, and as indicated in 12:11, "They overcame him [Satan] because of the blood of the Lamb and because of the word of their testimony."

Verses 5-8

The temple of the tabernacle of testimony in heaven is opened and the seven angels with the seven plagues come out of the temple. One of the four living creatures gives them seven golden bowls full of the wrath of God. The temple is filled with smoke from the glory of God and no one can enter the temple until the seven plagues are finished.

When on earth, the tabernacle contained the ark of the covenant (often called the ark of the testimony because it contained the two stone tablets on which God had given the Ten Commandments to Moses). The ark had a gold cover with golden cherubim at each end facing the center; the center portion of the cover was called the "mercy seat" because the Israelites considered it to be God's throne. The ark of His covenant was disclosed in Revelation 11:19 as being in the temple that opened in heaven, which was considered to be God's dwelling place. It is apparent, therefore, that the angels coming out of the temple come from the presence of God with instructions to proceed with the execution of

God's judgments issued by the court. Until the angels finish dispensing the wrath of God contained in the seven bowls, the temple is filled with the smoke of God's glory, and the temple with the ark and the mercy seat is closed. God would now be dealing in judgment and not mercy. As Paul observed in Hebrews 10:29-31, for those who reject God's Son, it will be "a terrifying thing to fall into the hands of the living God."

REVELATION 16

Verses 1-2

A loud voice from the temple tells the angels to get on with their work of pouring the contents of the seven bowls on the earth. This seems to be the voice of God coming from the temple. As these angels proceed with their duties, we should remember that they are unseen on earth but the results of their activities are seen. The people of earth wonder about these *unnatural* natural events that are taking place primarily in Israel and the Middle East.

The first angel pours out his bowl into the earth and it results in loathsome sores on those who have the mark of the beast and who worship his image. Recall that in 13:16, the second beast (or false prophet) required everyone to receive the "mark" on their forehead or right hand in order to buy or sell. The false prophet also required that everyone worship the image of the beast that had been created, under penalty of death for not doing so. In chapter 15, John saw in heaven those who had been victorious over the beast, which, as discussed there, indicated that they had been killed. As discussed earlier it is my opinion that both the "mark" and worship of the image were probably imposed primarily on the Jewish people and the surrounding nations. Most of those who remain in Israel and the Middle East, and have not been killed by one of the previous ordeals, have most probably worshiped the image of the beast or been imprinted with his mark under these decrees. Therefore, nearly all would be affected by the plague, but it would be limited in its application. This plague of "loathsome and malignant" sores will be much like the plague of boils sent against Egypt to persuade Pharaoh to release the Jews (Exodus 9:8-12). This time, however, the plague will come against the Jews, as had been promised if they disobeyed God (Deuteronomy 28:27, 35).

Verses 3-7

Apparently the remaining six plagues are administered in rapid succession, for the second follows the first without delay in John's vision. The second plague contaminates the sea as it becomes blood (note that it is not *like* blood, but *is* blood) and all things living in the sea are killed. The third angel closely follows the second, and his plague turns rivers and springs (fresh water) to blood. This is followed by a rather unusual set of events as the angel of waters both approves and justifies these two judgments. He praises God's righteousness in judging these things, indicating that God is justified because those judged had poured out the blood of saints and prophets, so they deserve getting blood to drink.

This declaration by the angel seems to indicate that these water judgments are poured out only on those who killed the saints and prophets. These judgments may, therefore, have been limited in geographic scope to the country of Israel, for it was the scribes and Pharisees whom Christ blamed for killing the saints and prophets. In Matthew 23:27-36 and again in Luke 11:45-50, Christ's message to the scribes and Pharisees was that they were hypocrites, a brood of vipers, the sons of those who killed the prophets and apostles, and that they were witness to and approved of the deeds of their fathers. Christ said, "For this reason also the wisdom of God said, 'I will send to them prophets and apostles, and some of them they will kill and some they will persecute, in order that the blood of all the prophets, shed since the foundation of the world, may be charged against this generation, from the blood of Abel to the blood of Zechariah'" (Luke 11:49-51).

So it seems that when the angel says, "They poured out the blood of saints and prophets," he is referring to these accusations that Christ charged against the Jews, thereby indicating that this judgment will fall on the Jews.

The angel's statement is followed by the altar saying, "Yes, O Lord God, the Almighty, true and righteous are your judgments." It appears that, since the altar could not speak, the comments coming from the altar are probably from those souls that are under the altar and who had cried for vengeance in 6:10. As discussed in chapter 6, it seems that these are the souls of Jewish people who had been killed during the tribulation; however, some of them may very well be those prophets and saints from ages past to which the angel (and Christ) referred. By the praise these souls give to God from the altar, it seems that the judgments administered by the angels will satisfy them.

From both the angel's comment and the comments from the altar, it seems an obvious conclusion that these judgments are solely on the Jewish nation. The text seems to imply that those in heaven can observe these judgments being administered.

The action of the second angel (who turned the sea to blood) has no Egyptian counterpart; however, the action of the third angel (who turned the fresh water of rivers and springs into blood) is similar to the first plague that Moses employed against the Egyptians when he turned the Nile River into blood (Exodus 7:14-25).

Verses 8-9

The fourth angel immediately releases the contents of his bowl upon the sun, causing the heat to intensify and resulting in people being scorched with the extreme heat. This does not cause people to repent, however; instead, they blaspheme the name of God, who has control over these plagues. There are some, however, who have to endure this bowl and are faithful. The great multitude that John saw in chapter 7 came out of the great tribulation (7:14) and John was told they would neither hunger nor thirst, nor will the sun beat down on them, nor any heat (7:16), presumably referring to this plague and indicating that some of those saved went through it.

There are a few Old Testament references that may be referring to this judgment, but it cannot be said for certain. For example, in Isaiah 24:6, Isaiah indicated that the inhabitants of the earth will be burned and few men will be left. In Deuteronomy 28:22-23, part of the warning about the curses that will fall on Israel for disobeying God included fiery heat, a sky of bronze, and an earth of iron (indicating drought due to heat and lack of rain). There is no Egyptian counterpart to this judgment, nor is there an exact parallel in the trumpet judgments. The only indication that this judgment of searing heat has any geographic limitation is the Deuteronomy 28 reference to curses that will fall on Israel. This may also be a judgment only on Israel.

Verses 10-11

The "fifth angel poured out his bowl upon the throne of the beast; and his kingdom became darkened." The people are in agonizing pain, and they blaspheme God because of their pains and sores—but they do not repent.

In 13:2, Satan gave the beast his throne. If the throne of the beast is, as surmised in that chapter, the area included in Alexander's empire, then this judgment will be limited to those nations that are part of the antichrist's kingdom—namely Iraq, Iran, Afghanistan, Pakistan, Syria, Turkey, Jordan and possibly several other Muslim countries of the Middle East. This plague is similar to the plague of darkness visited on Egypt (Exodus 10:21-29), and could also be the event referred to in Joel 2:30-31, Matthew 24:29, and several other scriptures that speak of the last days when the sun and moon will be darkened.

Verse 12

The sixth angel pours out his bowl upon the Euphrates River and dries it up to prepare the way for the kings from the east. This bowl has been the subject of many interpretations. Possibly the most popular has been the speculation that the two-hundred-million-man army (mentioned in 9:16) is an army from China and the drying up of the Euphrates paves the way for the army into the Middle East and Israel

The logic of this assumption is questionable. A review of the map of this area discloses that there are a great many more obstacles beside the Euphrates River between China and Israel that would be even more difficult to overcome. For instance, the Tigris River, which is east of the

Euphrates and is between China and Israel, is not mentioned as being dried up, so why is the Euphrates specifically named? As indicated in the discussion of this army of two hundred million in chapter 9, it is unlikely that it is a human army; if it were, there would be no need to dry up the Euphrates in order for it to pass, considering today's weaponry and equipment. Drying up the Euphrates may have something to do with the third bowl that turned water into blood resulting in an impassable river, or at least one in which normal bridging operations will be of no value. The reference to preparing the way for the kings of the East probably refers to the ten kingdoms under control of the antichrist. The kings of the world are also part of the sixth bowl and are discussed below, but there is no apparent reason to believe that this judgment has anything to do with China, India, Japan, or other nations of the Far East.

Verses 13-14

Immediately following the drying up of the river, John sees a science-fiction like scene as unclean spirits of demons, like frogs, come out of the mouths of the unholy trinity: the dragon, the beast, and the false prophet. The demons waste no time as they perform signs, which are some kind of seducing message to the kings of the whole world in order to gather them together for the war of the "great day of God, the Almighty." This is probably the event recorded in Joel 3, the time when God calls the nations together in the valley of Jehoshaphat for His judgment. It is doubtful that these unclean spirits can be seen by humans, but they are visible to John and are certainly under the control of the antichrist.

These demons go out to the kings of "the whole world." According to Herbert Lockyer's *Illustrated Dictionary of the Bible*, the Old Testament definition of "world" extended from Spain to Persia and from Greece to Ethiopia. The New Testament version included the southern portion of the Roman Empire, which I presume included Italy and all those nations around the southern shore of the Mediterranean Sea. If these are the limitations of John's "world" in these visions of the "whole world," then the world to which these demons go would include only the nations around the Mediterranean Sea and those east of Israel up through Persia (Iran). Geographically this would include much of Alexander's empire and would also include the ten kingdoms that are under control of the antichrist and where his throne is located.

This limited definition of John's "world" is probably most logical. The armies of the whole world, consisting of hundreds of nations of Europe, North and South America, Asia, Africa, and Oceania would probably need more space than all of Israel to be congregated. That the whole world includes only those nations around the Mediterranean seems also to be consistent with Daniel's interpretation of Nebuchadnezzar's vision of the great statue. In that vision, the ten toes were struck and destroyed by the stone cut out without hands (Daniel 2:34). In Daniel's vision of the four beasts and ten horns in chapter 7, we are told in that text that the ten horns are ten kings and another horn or king (the antichrist) will arise and take over three of them. After a time of mischief, "the court will sit for judgment" (Daniel 7:26), the antichrist will be destroyed, and the kingdom consisting of the ten kings and the antichrist will be destroyed forever.

In Joel 3, God spoke of the time that He will restore Judah and Jerusalem. He will gather all the nations to the valley of Jehoshaphat, and He will enter His judgment with the nations there. In Joel 3:11-12, God says, "Hasten and come, all you surrounding nations, and gather yourselves there. Bring down, O LORD, Thy mighty ones. Let the nations be aroused and come up to the valley of Jehoshaphat, for there I will sit to judge all the surrounding nations." In these passages He refers to the "surrounding" nations, which gives an impression that He is talking about those close to Israel rather than those that are far distant.

It appears that when these passages in Daniel and Joel are compared, they do describe the same series of events and the battle of Armageddon. Both of the visions in Daniel include ten kings and in Joel include the surrounding nations that are defeated at Christ's return. It seems, therefore, that these armies are limited to ten kings and do not include hundreds of kings to be defeated at His coming.

The mystery is why the kings are called together and how many of them are there? The text is specific that the kings are called together by the demons for the war of the "great day of God." Joel says God calls the nations together, but here, as more detail is provided, it is seen that God uses the demons for this purpose.

Verses 15-16

Although the demons do this task, it is doubtful that they realize that they are calling these kings together to wage war against God's armies, because the timing of the Lord's coming would not be known by them. This is emphasized in verse 15 as Christ announces that He is coming "like a thief," that is, unexpectedly. Similar comments that His coming will be like a "thief" are found in Matthew 24:43, 1 Thessalonians 5:2, 2 Peter 3:10, and Revelation 3:3. These "thief" verses are used by many as being related to the rapture, but certainly at the time of verse 15, the rapture has already occurred. He adds to this warning a blessing, the third one in Revelation, for the one who stays awake and keeps his garments, so he won't walk around naked and men see his shame. This passage is rather obscure, presumably related to Christ's coming. It is, of course, directed to believers who are alive at that time and strongly suggests that they be alert. When they see this gathering of forces around Jerusalem, they should expect the Lord's second coming at any time. The comment regarding clothes may mean that the lack of understanding and awareness in the gathering of forces around Jerusalem would leave them as unprepared for the Lord's return as are unbelieving men, thereby being ashamed of their unpreparedness as if they had been caught without clothes.

Christ not only warns of His coming like a thief, but certainly implies that His coming correlates to the gathering of Satan and his forces. Most commentators attribute this gathering of armies to either a rebellion against the antichrist who most feel controls the world, or possibly a civil war between the various nations. In either of these scenarios, the opinion is that they all forget their original cause and focus on the Lord when He appears.

It seems to me that there can only be one reason that would bring these kings together, and that is to enhance the primary purpose of the antichrist—to attack and finally destroy Israel. Here, again, the Old Testament throws light on this scene. Zechariah 14 appears to chronicle the same event that is in Revelation 16, the battle of Armageddon. The subject of the nations of the earth coming against Jerusalem was begun in Zechariah 12, but in 14:2 God said, "I will gather all the nations against Jerusalem to battle." The battle is described and Jerusalem is captured, then Zechariah wrote in 14:3-4, "Then the LORD will go forth and fight against those nations, as when He fights on a day of battle. And in that day His feet will stand on the Mount of Olives, which is in front of Jerusalem on the east; and the Mount of Olives will be split in its middle from east to west by a very large valley." In the latter part of 14:5 He states, "Then the LORD, my God, will come, and all the holy ones with Him!"—just as described in Revelation 19:11-14.

The remainder of Zechariah 14 describes this event in further detail with three matters of interest I would like to point out. The first is in Zechariah 14:6 where it says that "there will be no light" on this day. This may be the darkness that was poured out by the fifth angel on the throne of the beast. As discussed earlier, I believe the "throne" refers to the countries that made up Alexander's empire which surround Israel, most of which are east of Jerusalem. The "day of the LORD" is described in several scriptures as being a day of darkness (see Joel 2:2; 3:15; and Zephaniah 1:15).

The second matter is in Zechariah 14:12 where it is noted that those warring against Jerusalem are struck by a plague which rots their flesh, their eyes, and their tongues while they stand on their feet. The seven bowls in Revelation 15:8 are referred to as seven "plagues."

The final comment of interest is in Zechariah 14:14-16, which states that the wealth of the surrounding nations will be gathered by Jerusalem, and that any people who are left of all the nations that fought against Jerusalem, with particular emphasis on Egypt, will come each year to worship the Lord at the Feast of Booths. Here, as in Joel 3 (referred to earlier), the scripture speaks of the "surrounding" nations, and makes a point of Egypt, which again appears to infer that the nations involved will be largely Middle Eastern nations.

Verse 16 indicates that the destination of the gathered forces is a place called Har-Magedon, or in Greek, Armageddon. This is the only place that this location is mentioned in the Bible. It is generally thought to refer to the mountain of Megiddo which is on the edge of the valley of Jezreel, sometimes referred to as the plain of Esdraelon, lying between Mount Carmel and the city of Jezreel. There have been several battles in this location (see Judges 6:33; 1 Samuel 29:1), but it is not of sufficient area to hold all the armies of the world. It could be a staging area, however, for the armies of the beast (including his ten nations) before their attack on Jerusalem.

Verses 17-21

The seventh angel pours his bowl out into the air and a loud voice from the throne announces: "It is done." With this, there is an eruption of nature as lightning, thunder, huge hailstones weighing one hundred pounds each, and the greatest earthquake that has ever occurred on earth destroys cities, floods islands, levels mountains, and splits the great city (Jerusalem) into three parts. Among these activities God does not forget to level His wrath against Babylon, and men blaspheme God because the plague of hail is extremely severe. These convolutions of the earth were included in the end time prophecies recorded in Joel 2:10 and 3:16; Haggai 2:6-9; and Zechariah 14:5.

REVELATION 17

Chapters 17 and 18 are dedicated to a description of the destruction of Babylon. One of the seven angels involved with God's final judgments directs John's attention to the judgment of the "great harlot who sits on many waters."

Many expositors believe that the harlot represents false religions that have been in existence since the time of Babel and that the false religions have been supported and protected by the nations that composed the kingdoms of the seven beasts we have discussed. Regarding the harlot John observes, the expositors suggest that the woman represents the final form of the apostate church spoken of in 2 Thessalonians 2:3, "It [the day of Lord] will not come unless the apostasy comes first." The assumption that the woman represents the apostasy of the last days has some merit because after the rapture, the many mainline and other Christian churches will be left with only those members who adhere to the New Age theology that already prevails in many of them today. Apostasy is a falling away from the faith and not a heathen religious system such as the Babylonian religious system. After the rapture and the removal of the restrainer, there will undoubtedly be an apostate religion of those who retain the name of Christ but not the spirit as referred to in 2 Thessalonians 2. In addition, there will be the false prophet requiring everyone to worship the image of the antichrist. Either of these religions could be in control of this beast just as Islam appears to control many nations today.

I do not find any evidence in scripture that this woman represents a religious system. Some consider that the reference in verses 2 and 3 to acts of immorality supply the evidence that she represents an apostate system that bears God's name but worships other gods. Verse 18, however, indicates that "the woman whom you saw is the great city, which reigns over the kings of the earth," so she does not represent a religious system. Then 18:7, "she glorified herself and lived sensuously," implies that her immoralities are the glorifying of herself and sensuous living. Both of these lifestyle characteristics indicate a worldly, materialistic, personal gratification, and ungodly lifestyle for a city, a nation, or a people.

Verses 1-6

The angel who comes to speak to John describes this woman in the following ways:

(1) She sits on many waters (verse 1). In 17:15, John is told that waters where she sits "are peoples and multitudes and nations and tongues."

(2) Kings of the earth commit acts of immorality with her (verse 2).

(3) Those dwelling on the earth are made drunk with the wine of her immorality (verse 2).

(4) She is in a wilderness sitting on a scarlet beast that is full of blasphemous names and has seven heads and ten horns (verse 3).

(5) She is clothed in purple and scarlet—both of these colors denote royalty, wealth, and could also appear to be certain ecclesiastical robes, indicating status (verse 4).

(6) She is adorned with gold, precious stones, and pearls—certainly these items denote wealth (verse 4).

(7) She holds in her hand a gold cup full of abominations and of the unclean things of her immorality. This indicates idolatry (verse 4).

(8) On her forehead is written a mysterious name, "BABYLON THE GREAT, THE MOTHER OF HARLOTS AND OF THE ABOMINATIONS OF THE EARTH" (verse 5).

(9) She is drunk with the blood of the saints and with the blood of the witnesses of Jesus (verse 6).

Verses 7-8

John expresses wonder at what he was seeing, and the angel says, "Why do you wonder? I shall tell you the mystery." However, the angel's explanation seems to create an even larger mystery.

The angel states that the beast "was and is not," and "is about to come up out of the abyss and go to destruction." Those on earth whose names had not been written in the book of life will wonder when they see the beast.

So who is this beast? It has the same identifying characteristics as the dragon in chapter 12, which was identified as Satan, and the beast in chapter 13, which was identified as the antichrist. In both cases, the identifiers were the seven heads, the ten horns, and the blasphemous names. In addition, the dragon, or Satan, was colored red. This beast is scarlet, a dark red (verse 3). His color was probably the result of Satan transferring his power, throne, and authority to the beast. The transfer of these major aspects of his personality by Satan could hardly be accomplished without also transferring the dark red complexion mentioned in this scene.

This beast is apparently the same one described in chapter 13, meaning this beast is the antichrist (who has the power of Satan). Recall that in that chapter, one of the beast's seven heads appeared as if it had been slain but was healed, and the people were so amazed they began to worship the beast (the antichrist). Here the beast "was and is not, and is about to come up out of the abyss" (verse 8). Here's how I make the connection: The antichrist will apparently be well known in the world after the restrainer is removed. He will enter into a covenant with the Jews. He will be involved in some battles and probably will be killed in Jerusalem (Daniel 11:45) at the end of the first three-and-a-half years of his reign. He then will come from the abyss (come back from death), probably possessed by a demon. He will appear to be healed and will conduct Satan's business, including making war with the saints and killing the two witnesses (Revelation 11:7). So, as seen in chapter 17, he "was" (lives and reigns for three-and-a-half years), he "is not" (is killed in battle in Jerusalem), and "is about to come up out of the abyss" (appears healed).

"Those who dwell on the earth will wonder, whose name has not been written in the book of life from the foundation of the world, when they see the beast, that he was and is not and will come." This reaction is very similar to the worship described in chapter 13, leading to the conclusion that it is the same scene and the same beast as in chapter 13, and (also as discussed in the commentary on chapter 13), it is also the fourth beast in Daniel's vision in Daniel 7. It appears that the re-emergence of the beast from the abyss will occur at the beginning of the last three-and-a-half-year period of the tribulation.

Verses 9-11

The angel then tells John that "the seven heads are seven mountains on which the woman sits, and they are seven kings; five have fallen, one is, the other has not yet come; and when he comes, he must remain a little while. The angel continues, saying that the beast is himself one of the seven and is also an eighth.

There are various thoughts by expositors as to the meaning of the seven mountains. The one most accepted is that they refer to the seven hills of Rome; this fits the conclusion that the antichrist will arise from a revived Roman Empire, and Rome will be the center of his reign. Others believe that the mountains are kingdoms. This is strongly implied by the phrase, "they are seven kings." Scripture also supports the conclusion that these mountains refer to kingdoms because the word *mountain* is used in other prophecies to refer to a nation or kingdom. For example, Isaiah 2:2 speaks of the "mountain of the house of the LORD" being chief of all mountains, referring to nations. Daniel 2:35 speaks of the stone that struck Nebuchadnezzar's statue becoming a "great mountain" that fills the whole earth. This mountain is Christ's millennial kingdom.

This beast has seven heads, which, as noted above, I believe refer to seven kingdoms. Four of these seven kingdoms are referred to in Zechariah 1:18-21,

Then I lifted up my eyes and looked, and behold, there were four horns. So I said to the angel who was speaking with me, "What are these?" And he answered me, "These are the horns which have scattered Judah, Israel and Jerusalem." Then the LORD showed me four craftsmen. I said, "What are these coming to do?" And he said, "These are the horns which have scattered Judah so that no man lifts up his head; but these craftsmen have come to terrify them, to throw down the horns of the nations who have lifted up their horns against the land of Judah in order to scatter it."

This passage in Zechariah also gives insight into God's meaning when He uses the term "horns." The angel, who had been speaking to Zechariah about the Lord returning to Jerusalem with compassion and building His house, showed him four horns. The angel explained that these were the nations that had scattered Judah, Israel, and Jerusalem; they had raised their horns against the land of Judah and would be thrown down.

These four horns in Zechariah have been identified by some commentators as four of the world's major empires—Egypt, Assyria, Babylonia, and Medo-Persia. Four of the heads in Revelation 17 have been similarly identified. And these four all have "fallen" or been thrown down as predicted in the Zechariah passage. The fifth kingdom in Revelation 17, which had not yet been part of history in Zechariah's time, was Greece—and that empire too has fallen, making the five that have already fallen, as the angel said. The "one" that "is" refers to the sixth kingdom that was in existence at the time John wrote Revelation—the Roman Empire. The seventh, which "must remain a little while" will be the first three-and-a-half year reign of the beast, the antichrist. He is "himself also an eighth" kingdom because he would be killed, would appear to be healed, and then would reign for another three-and-a-half years, becoming the eighth kingdom by virtue of his re-emergence. He is an eighth kingdom, but is actually "one of the seven." These are the five that have fallen, the one that is, and the one that is yet to come that will also be the eighth kingdom.

All seven (eight) of these kingdoms have had or will have dominion over Israel. It appears, therefore, that the body of the beast is the commonality of these kingdoms' dominance over Israel. This dominance has been exercised, however, by several authorities or kings or kingdoms, which have been reflected as seven heads. The horns are also kings, but a special kind according to Zechariah. They have raised their horns against and participated in the scattering of Judah, Israel, and Jerusalem.

Verses 12-18

The angel then refers to the other characters who are on stage at this point—the ten horns. These represent ten kings "who have not yet received a kingdom, but they receive authority as kings with the beast for one hour. These have one purpose and they give their power and authority to the beast" to wage war against the Lamb.

The Lamb will overcome them for He is the Lord of lords and King of kings, but before He does, the beast and the ten kings destroy the harlot whom they hate and burn her with fire, "for God has put it in their hearts to execute His purpose," until His word should be fulfilled. It is said these ten "will destroy" the woman, which implies that it will occur after this vision. The ten horns are called kings, but apparently they are not truly kings since they "have not yet received a kingdom." Possibly they are "kings" in name only, merely representatives of member countries to the federation of ten nations headed up by the antichrist. However, they do have enough authority to commit their countries to the service of the beast.

"And the woman whom you saw is the great city, which reigns over the kings of the earth" (17:18). This statement, combined with the nine descriptive phrases noted earlier in verses 2 through 6, present an unsolved mystery in the identification of the woman that John sees sitting on the beast. I do not accept the theory that she represents an ecclesiastical system.

REVELATION 18

Verses 1-2

After those things John saw in chapter 17, he next sees another angel coming down from heaven crying out in a mighty voice, "Fallen, fallen, is Babylon the great! And she has become a dwelling place of demons and a prison of every unclean spirit, and a prison of every unclean and hateful bird."

Is this the same Babylon of chapter 17? I believe it is. Many commentators, however, suggest that chapter 18 describes a different event than does chapter 17. They believe that chapter 17 describes either the apostate church or a political system, and chapter 18 describes an economic system. Many commentators also contend that since the two chapters are announced by different angels, and that the Babylon of chapter 18 is mourned and the one in chapter 17 is not mourned, means that they must be different entities. There is also considerable opinion that the Babylon of chapter 18 is the ancient city of Babylon that has been rebuilt.

In comparing the two chapters, it appears to me that they are speaking about the same entity, not two separate ones. There are several similarities in the references to Babylon that would indicate they are the same Babylon. The angel who made the announcement in 18:2, is probably the same one who announced in 14:8 the fall of Babylon the great, saying, "she who has made all the nations drink of the wine of the passion of her immorality." This same description is used in 17:2, and again in 18:2. Another similar reference is in both 17:2 and 18:3 where it is said that "the kings of the earth committed acts of immorality" with her. Then 18:16 actually repeats 17:4. The clothing of "fine linen and purple and scarlet," and adornment of "gold and precious stones and pearls," first mentioned in 17:4, is described in 18:17 as "such great wealth." Therefore, it is my conclusion that these items are meant to describe the wealth of the woman, and not her ecclesiastical affiliation as some have claimed. I believe that all of these references relate to the same entity, and that entity is neither the apostate church nor the rebuilt city of Babylon.

As we saw in chapter 17, John used the word *will* when referring to the destruction of the woman (Babylon) in 17:16, "These *will* hate the harlot and *will* make her desolate and naked, and *will* eat her flesh and *will* burn her up with fire" (italics mine). In chapter 18, the destruction has not yet occurred for the angel continues to use the word *will* (see 18: 8, 9, 15, 21, 22, 23). Since her destruction is yet future, then the angel's message: "Fallen, fallen is Babylon," must be in reference to her relationship with God and not her physical destruction. In other words, she has fallen from God's grace. It does appear that she has had a change of character, in that she has "become" a place where demons and every unclean spirit dwell.

Verses 3-8

According to verse 3, all the nations of the earth have participated with her sensual living: the kings on one level, presumably politically or financially; and on another level, the merchants of the earth contributed to her sinful ways and became rich by selling their goods to her. Further indications that the destruction has not begun is the voice John hears in verses 4 and 5, announcing, "Come out of her, my people, that you may not participate in her sins and that you may not receive of her plagues; for her sins have piled up as high as heaven."

It seems she has offended God greatly as she is to be paid back double according to her deeds. She has glorified herself, lived sensually, and believed in her heart that she was a queen that would never be judged or see mourning. She was arrogant.

In verse 8, the angel announces that for this reason she will be judged and her plagues will come in one day—pestilence, mourning, famine, and then she will be burned up with fire for the God who judges her is strong. Referring back to 17:16, it was indicated that God would put it in the hearts of the beast and ten kings to execute His purpose and destroy the harlot, so He will use them as His servants to exercise this judgment.

Verses 9-19

Verses 9 through 19 describe the effect that Babylon's destruction will have on the world of commerce.

Verse 9: The kings of the earth, who committed acts of immorality and lived sensuously with her, will weep and lament when they see the smoke of her burning.

Verse 10: From a distance, they mourn the destruction of the great, strong city. In one hour, her judgment had come.

Verse 11: Merchants of the earth also mourn due to the loss of a great customer.

Verses 12-13: These verses list the types goods Babylon bought from the merchants, most of them denoting luxury; she also traded in slaves and human lives.

Verses 15-17: Again the merchants, who became rich from her, will mourn and weep saying, "Woe, woe, the great city, she who was clothed in fine linen and purple and scarlet, and adorned with gold and precious stones and pearls; for in one hour such great wealth has been laid waste!" And those that make a living at sea observed from a distance.

Verse 18: They said, "What city is like the great city?"

Verse 19: They mourned her because all who had ships at sea became rich in trading with her.

Verses 20-24

Verse 20 indicates that there is rejoicing in heaven by the saints, apostles, and prophets because God has pronounced judgment for them against her. Then an angel threw a great millstone into the sea to illustrate how Babylon, the great city, will "be thrown down with violence, and will not be found any longer." There will no longer be any joyful or normal living activity in her—no more musicians making melodies, no more craftsmen making their crafts, no more workers doing their daily tasks, no more weddings, no one will even light a lamp. Her destruction will be complete because "in her was found the blood of prophets and of saints and of all who had been slain on the earth."

A NOTE ON BABYLON THE GREAT

Once again we pause in proceeding in Revelation to discuss one of the principal entities in Scripture. Who is this woman on the beast, this harlot, and why is she such a problem? Why is God so extremely displeased with her?

The first matter to be addressed is the nature of this woman. She is referred to as a great city that reigns over the kings of the earth (17:18). Many believe that this refers to Rome as the head of the apostate church. Many others believe that this is rebuilt Babylon. This opinion received a lot of attention several years ago when it was found that Saddam Hussein was actually beginning a project to rebuild the city which had not been completed when he was detained and probably never will be. I do not consider either of these theories to be an acceptable identification of this woman.

The first question to be answered: Is Babylon a city? Again we go to the Old Testament for help. Jeremiah 50 and 51 are Jeremiah's prophecies against Babylon, one of many foreign nations that are enemies of Judah. The "cities" of Babylon are mentioned in 50:32 and 51:43 (note the reference to more than one city); 50:32 indicates that God shall set fire to the cities, 51:43 says, "Her cities have become an object of horror." There are other indications that Babylon is not one city, but rather an entire nation. It is obvious from the grief exhibited by shipmasters and sailors at Babylon's fall (which we read about in chapter 18) that material goods had reached her by ship. A new city of Babylon built on the site of the old city could not be reached by an ocean-going vessel or even by barge on the Euphrates River. This is seen today by the need for the military to unload supplies to be delivered to Baghdad at the Kuwait port on the Gulf of Oman.

Furthermore, the grief of the sailors and merchants indicates that the fall of Babylon has an extreme economic impact on the economy of the world. Considering the size of the world's current economic output, there is no city that has such a large consumption that its destruction would have such a dramatic impact upon the economy of the world. This includes all of the great cities such as New York, London, or Tokyo. It appears, therefore, that Babylon must refer to a nation and not a single city.

The scriptural clues to the identification of Babylon are numerous and, based upon our belief that the time of the Lord's return is near this Babylon should be a nation in existence at the time and the identification of Babylon the great should be fairly certain. I have identified these clues as follows:

(1) Revelation 17:1—*Babylon sits on many waters.* Verse 15 states that the waters represent "peoples and multitudes and nations and tongues." This is comparable to 17:18, the woman is "the great city, which reigns over the kings of the earth." Jeremiah 50:23 speaks of the destruction of Babylon by saying that "the hammer of the whole earth has been cut off and broken." All of these references indicate that she controls (sits on) many nations, but does not rule any of them. She apparently controls with coercive power, which could be either economic or military. Jeremiah 51:13 speaks to the same status, "O you who dwell by many waters…your end has come."

(2) Revelation 17:2, 18:3, and Jeremiah 51:7—*Babylon is immoral and glorifies herself.* Those on the earth were made drunk with the wine of her immorality and the kings of the earth committed acts of immorality with her. Her immorality was her sensual living and the glorifying of herself (Revelation 18:7).

(3) Revelation 17:4 and 18:16-17—*Babylon is extremely wealthy* Jeremiah 50:37 refers to her treasures being plundered and 51:13 says she is abundant in treasures, but 51:7, is of the most interest as it states, "Babylon has been a golden cup in the hand of the LORD, intoxicating all the earth." Note the tense, she "has been" used by the Lord as a

golden cup. Apparently He had used her wealth for His own purposes, but ultimately that wealth intoxicated the rest of the world.

(4) Revelation 18:9-19—*Babylon's destruction will be greatly mourned.* The kings of the earth, the merchants, and those who transport both goods and passengers by ship, weep and mourn at the destruction of Babylon. Jeremiah 50:46 also hints at this distress as it claims, "At the shout, 'Babylon has been seized!' the earth is shaken, and an outcry is heard among the nations."

(5) Revelation 18:4—*God will call His people out of Babylon.* God calls His people out of her "that you may not participate in her sins and that you may not receive of her plagues." In Jeremiah 51:6, the Israelites are told to "flee from the midst of Babylon," and again in 51:45 God says, "Come forth from her midst, My people, and each of you save yourselves from the fierce anger of the LORD"

(6) Revelation 18:6-7—*Babylon will be paid back for her great sin-*fulness. She is to receive double what she put out all because of her arrogance. She says in her heart, "I SIT AS A QUEEN AND I AM NOT A WIDOW, and will never see mourning." In Jeremiah 50:29, the same ideas are expressed: "Repay her according to her work; according to all that she has done, so do to her."

(7) Jeremiah 50:29—*Babylon at one time recognized the Lord, but she became arrogant.* "She has become arrogant against the LORD, against the Holy One of Israel." It appears that Babylon had once recognized the Lord, for here it mentions that she "has become" arrogant, indicating that it had not always been so.

(8) There are a number of other identifiers in Jeremiah that are not mentioned in Revelation:

Jeremiah 50:12—*Babylon has a mother who is still existent.*

Jeremiah 50:37—*Foreigners live in her midst.*

Jeremiah 50:42—*This Babylon is not the original Babylon.* She is described as the "daughter" of Babylon, referring to her as an offspring.

Jeremiah 51:53—*Babylon has lofty strongholds, such as space defenses.*

Jeremiah 51:55—*Babylon is the source of loud noise* that the Lord will make vanish.

(9) Revelation 17:3—*Babylon will exercise control over ten nations, and those nations will not like it.* The woman was sitting on a scarlet beast that was full of blasphemous names and had seven heads and ten horns. The beast was discussed earlier. He represents the nations that have dominated Israel since Egypt. The beast's seven heads, or kingdoms, are apparently still alive since they appear mounted on this beast. That is in accord with Nebuchadnezzar's vision of the statue that was one seamless representation of a king, even though it represented several kingdoms, and they were all destroyed at one time by the stone cut out of the mountain without hands (Daniel 2:31-45). The ten horns are the ten-nation confederacy that is headed up by the last of the beast's seven heads. The seventh head is otherwise known as the antichrist. The woman (defined in 17:5 as "BABYLON THE GREAT, THE MOTHER OF HARLOTS AND OF THE ABOMINATIONS OF THE EARTH") is sitting on these ten nations and is exercising a control which they do not appreciate, for according to 17:16, they hate her and ultimately destroy her.

The entity that fits practically all of those identifiers listed above is the United States of America.

Item 1— Babylon sits on many waters The U.S. sits on many waters or nations, if not most of the world, and exercises influence over the whole world either diplomatically, by her position in the United Nations, or by coercion with her military power.

Item 2—Babylon is immoral and glorifies herself. Practically all of the nations of the earth have in one way or another participated in the wealth of the U.S. by selling their goods to her or have asked and received loans or subsidies, thereby committing acts of immorality with her by becoming dependent on her continued economic well being for their own future rather than depending on God.

Item 3—Babylon is extremely wealthy The material wealth of the U.S. is greater than any nation in the history of the world. All nations have wanted to and have participated in that wealth, and many have become rich. Her wealth has been the result of the Lord's blessing and she has been a golden cup in His hand. More missionaries have been sent out into the world from the U.S. than from any other nation. There have been more churches, more schools, more hospitals established in the name of the Lord Jesus in the U.S. than anywhere else in the world. Of most importance, however, has been the protection and major assistance in establishing a nation for the Lord's chosen people, Israel. The Lord used the U.S., which He had built up over the past two hundred years, to establish and maintain that nation. The whole earth has become intoxicated with this materiality and her self-sufficiency that no longer gives acknowledgement or thanks to God for these blessings. Christ preached emphatically against dependence on riches because "where your treasure is, there will your heart be also," and He added that a person "cannot serve God and mammon [riches]." Apparently, according to Scripture, that is what Babylon decided to do: serve mammon before God.

Item 4—Babylon's destruction will be greatly mourned. Of particular interest is the distress of the shipmasters, sailors, and passengers. The only way the rest of the world can get quantities of goods to the U.S. is by ship, and our negative balance of payments (meaning we import much more than we export) has gotten so large that it is causing concern among economists and politicians. Should the U.S. be destroyed, the huge debt owed to other nations would not be repaid. This, in turn, would destroy their economies and cause distress among the nations.

Item 5—God will call His people out of Babylon. He wants them to avoid the punishment He is about to levy on her. The U.S. has the largest Jewish population of any other nation, including Israel.

Item 6— Babylon will be paid back for her great sinfulness. The punishment will come to her because she has become (note become, indicating she had not always been) arrogant against the Lord.

Item 7— Babylon at one time recognized the Lord, but she became arrogant. Although she may not yet be to that point in her relationship with the Lord, there have been complaints recently from the rest of the world about her arrogance.

*Item 8—*Regarding those identifiers that have only a Jeremiah reference, the United States fits all of them.

The United Kingdom or England is generally thought of as being the mother of the U.S. There are no other countries, of which I am aware, that are thought to have a mother.

There is no other country that has as many people who are not citizens who may be classified as foreign or alien as does the U.S. One of the matters of most concern at the present time is the question of how to control immigration and close the borders.

This Babylon is referred to as the daughter of Babylon. So this Babylon, in some way, resembles the early Babylon so closely that she is referred to as a daughter. This is probably a character trait, such as arrogance and pride, but could very well be her wealth and self-indulgent lifestyle.

She is spoken of as having lofty strongholds, which certainly fits the U.S. space technology and defenses, which no other nation has or can match.

She is spoken of as being a source of noise. No nation has ever been so noisy as the U.S. blasting her music and entertainment all over the world as well as her communication systems that are continually sending chatter into the airwaves.

Item 9— Babylon will exercise control over ten nations, and those nations will not like it. The ten-nation confederacy appears to be the revival of Alexander's empire of the Muslim nations rather than the revived Roman Empire. They are those nations over which the U.S. is currently exercising control (sitting on) either through military operations or negotiations with the threat of possible military action. Those nations currently in focus are Afghanistan, Iraq, Iran, Syria, and Saudi Arabia. The hate these nations presently express for the U.S. certainly makes 17:16 credible. The indication of her destruction by fire, in 17:16, 18:8-9 and 18:18-19, which will happen in "one hour" implies the use of nuclear weapons and could refer to the invasion of suicide bombers with nuclear weapons, which is currently one of our homeland security administrators' major concerns. The fact that God is motivating these people to carry out this destruction, as expressed in 17:17, would indicate that He would also prepare the way for the successful completion by blinding the anti-terrorism procedures of the U.S.

Another end time reference to the relationship between the antichrist and to one I believe is the U.S. is in Daniel 11:39. In that verse Daniel mentions that the antichrist "will take action against the strongest of fortresses." The U.S. is the mightiest nation that has ever existed and the various insurgencies are even now waging a campaign of terrorism against this country. Not a war, although President Bush considers it one, but they are taking action. Although the "strongest of fortresses" that Daniel has in mind is not identified as Babylon, it would be by inference if the U.S. alone fulfills both identities. The antichrist is not yet apparently in place, but such actions of terrorism could very well be continued under his reign and result in a final destruction by nuclear weapons. Iran is currently making quite an issue with the U.S. of continuing her pursuit of nuclear capability; again, this makes Revelation 17:16 credible and relevant.

That said, there are several references to Babylon that I find difficult to attribute to the United States, however I do not believe that they constitute sufficient doubt to negate the identification of the U.S. as the final Babylon. In Revelation 17:6, John sees the woman (Babylon), "drunk with the blood of the saints, and with the blood of the witnesses of Jesus." In 18:13, the list of commodities that are no longer bought by Babylon ends with "slaves and human lives." John ends chapter 18 with a terrible charge against Babylon, "And in her was found the blood of prophets and of saints and all who have been slain on the earth." A similar charge is summarily stated in Jeremiah 51:49, "Indeed Babylon is to fall for the slain of Israel, as also for Babylon the slain of all the earth have fallen."

These references are puzzling; however, there are certainly a few possible meanings that come to mind of which the U.S. has been guilty. The traffic in slaves was a major activity at one time and was an issue even at the time the Continental Congress addressed the language of the Constitution in 1787. The slavery concern continued to be a divisive issue in the country until settled by war from 1861–1865. The slaughter, through abortion, of some 43 million babies has been a recent atrocity of which we are all aware. As the epitome of and end of Gentile dominion of the earth and Israel, the U.S. may bear the blame for the atrocities of all previous Gentile nations.

As mentioned, there are two scriptures that imply that there has been a change in the character of this Babylon. In Jeremiah 51:7 Babylon is referred to as having been (past tense) a golden cup in the hand of the Lord; in Revelation 18:2 Babylon is said to have become (changed condition) a dwelling place of demons, unclean spirits, and unclean birds. If the U.S is that Babylon, as I believe, changes that will occur after the rapture of the church could be the cause of actions and attitudes, including the abandonment of Israel, for which God will condemn her to destruction. These attitudinal changes and actions that lead to God's anger may even be seen and projected from current developments within the religious, social, legal, and political structures of the nation. There are those, particularly in the A.C.L.U. and the courts, who are attempting to dismiss any acknowledgement of God from the conscience and fabric of the nation. Attorneys bring lawsuits and judges rule against any acknowledgement of God through the Ten Commandments, prayer in school, inclusion of creationism in text books, and any other public recognition of God. These court decisions are being made under the guise of a fictitious constitutional provision requiring that there be a separation between church and state.

REVELATION 19

Verses 1-3

John's next vision begins on a new note. It appears that Babylon has been destroyed, for there is rejoicing in heaven by a great multitude as they say, "Hallelujah! Salvation and glory and power belong to our God; BECAUSE HIS JUDGMENTS ARE TRUE AND RIGHTEOUS; for He has judged the great harlot who was corrupting the earth with her immorality, and HE HAS AVENGED THE BLOOD OF HIS BOND-SERVANTS ON HER" And a second time they said, "Hallelujah! HER SMOKE RISES UP FOREVER AND EVER." As those on earth could see the smoke arising from the attack on Babylon (18:17-18), so also can those in heaven.

Most students consider this multitude in chapter 19 to be those who were introduced in chapter 7 as the ones "who come out of the great tribulation" (7:14). As discussed in the study of that chapter, it appears that those are believers, due to their attitude of praise and their white robes that have been washed in the blood of the Lamb. These in chapter 19, however, are displaying the same attitude as did those under the altar in chapter 6 who were Jews and who were calling for revenge: "They cried out with a loud voice, saying, 'How long, O Lord, holy and true, wilt Thou refrain from judging and avenging our blood on those who dwell on the earth?'" (6:10). In chapter 19 they are praising God for avenging the blood of His bondservants. I suspect that these are the Jews of chapter 6 who are rejoicing at the destruction of Babylon.

Verses 4-8

In verse 4 it is noted that the twenty-four elders and the four living creatures (first introduced in chapter 4) fell down and worshiped God. Their attitude is more profound and solemn than the group mentioned in verse 1, for they are not animated at the destruction of Babylon; instead, the judgments which they observed have moved them to worship God. Although the twenty-four elders and the four living creatures did not experience the tribulation and the extremes of the antichrist's reign, they were, I believe, part of the court (Daniel 7:10, 26) who sat with God and Christ hearing the testimony against the antichrist and his followers. They were, presumably, those who passed final judgments (Revelation 20:4) and were fully aware of the terrible significance of their decision and its serious consequences on the inhabitants of the earth. They are awed by God's pronouncements and the execution of judgments on Israel, the earth, and the antichrist; they confirm those actions not with rejoicing but with a final resolve that terrible as the punishment was, it had to be, "Amen" or "so be it."

If the assumption is correct that the group referred to in verses 1-3 are the Jews from chapter 6, then neither the church which was raptured nor the tribulation saints introduced as the multitude in chapter 7 are represented in the display of emotion at the completion of the destruction of Babylon and the execution of judgments on the earth. Because the church had been raptured, it did not experience the satanic measures instituted by the antichrist and was not emotionally involved; indeed, they may be preoccupied by actively preparing for the marriage supper of the Lamb. The tribulation saints were praising God before the throne and were busy serving Him, according to chapter 7. So each of the four entities—(1) the twenty-four elders introduced in chapter 4, (2) the Jewish contingent introduced as being under the altar in chapter 6, (3) the church which was raptured, and (4) the tribulation saints introduced as the multitude in chapter 7—had a different response to the completion of God's destruction of Babylon.

The reaction to the destruction of Babylon is followed by an announcement from the throne that all those who fear God should praise Him, and a great multitude in heaven says, "Hallelujah! For the Lord our God, the Almighty, reigns." This praise is followed in verse 7 with the joyful announcement, "Let us rejoice and be glad and give the glory to Him, for the marriage of the Lamb has come and His bride has made herself ready." The bride is the church and as Paul told the Corinthians in 2 Corinthians 11:2, "I betrothed you to one husband, that to Christ I might present you as a pure virgin." This announcement was probably made by the tribulation saints, for the announcement speaks of the bride from the perspective of interested observers and not from a personal perspective. The tribulation saints are those in chapter 7 who came out of the great tribulation. They are not part of the church, but serve God day and night in His temple (Revelation 7:15) and the Lamb will be their shepherd and God will wipe away every tear from their eyes (7:17).

Verse 8 informs the reader how the bride has prepared herself: "It was given to her to clothe herself in fine linen, bright and clean; for the fine linen is the righteous acts of the saints." It seems these righteous acts were given to the church to sanctify her, thereby completing her separation from the world. She has responded to God's will in fulfilling those good works that He had prepared in advance (Ephesians 2:10) for her. This in keeping with Ephesians 5:25-27, "Husbands, love your wives, just as Christ also loved the church and gave Himself up for her; that He might sanctify her, having cleansed her by the washing of water with the word, that He might present to Himself the church in all her glory, having no spot or wrinkle or any such thing; but that she should be holy and blameless." And it should be noted that not only did He supply the blood in which she washed her robe, but He also promised the robe of white linen, which are the righteous acts of the saints.

Verses 9-10

John is then instructed to write, "Blessed are those who are invited to the marriage supper of the Lamb." This is the fourth beatitude (blessing) in Revelation. Then the angel tells John: "These are true words of God." Apparently this last phrase is necessary to emphasize that these are words actually uttered by God and not through one of His servants, the angels, and they express His personal feelings about the act of marriage. He gives His personal blessing to the marriage and, through it, blesses all who are invited to attend. Presumably this invitation did not include the bride as she is part of the ceremony, but did comprise all of the other inhabitants of heaven, which would refer to the Jewish contingent we have discussed as well as the tribulation saints.

Several commentators have emphasized how this marriage of Christ and the church followed Jewish tradition and custom in those days, so there is no need to add further discussion of those customs and how they further support the possibility of a rapture. There is also some discussion by commentators as to whether the event will take place in heaven or on earth. It does not seem to make too much difference as to where it takes place; however, the next few verses regarding Christ's return to earth at His second coming would seem to indicate that the marriage takes place in heaven, immediately after which Christ returns to take care of things on earth.

What I have found lacking in the discussion by commentators is any reflection on God's view of marriage, in that He considers marriage to be a permanent condition that binds the parties into one unity. This was set out in Genesis 2:24 before the advent of children and the fall of Adam, "For this cause a man shall leave his father and his mother, and shall cleave to his wife; and they shall become one flesh." This marriage may not be that of a man and a woman, but according to Paul in Ephesians 5:22-32, there is a great similarity between the marriage of a man and woman and the marriage of Christ and His church. In Ephesians 5:31 Paul quoted Genesis 2:24, and in verse 32 expanded on that passage, "This mystery is great; but I am speaking with reference to Christ and the church." The message seems to be that after the marriage supper of the Lamb, Christ and the church will in some way become one entity in the eyes of the Father. If so, it would seem that the position held by some that the church inherits the covenants God made with the Jews would not be valid, for the church will be one with Christ.

In verse 10, John fell at the feet of the angel who had been speaking to him, but the angel said he was not an appropriate subject for worship. He was just a fellow servant with John and his brethren who hold the testimony of Jesus, and they should worship God. Then the angel said, "For the testimony of Jesus is the spirit of prophecy." This statement confirms that all prophecy in Scripture, which includes the book of Revelation, is about Jesus. Some relative to His first advent, but as we know, all prophecy culminates in Christ's second coming.

Verses 11-16

As John looks, he sees heaven opened and he beholds

a white horse, and He who sat upon it is called Faithful and True; and in righteousness He judges and wages war. And His eyes are a flame of fire, and upon His head are many diadems, and He has a name written upon Him which no one knows except Himself. And He is clothed with a robe dipped in blood; and His name is called The Word of God.

This is the second coming of Christ. John goes on:

The armies which are in heaven, clothed in fine linen, white and clean, were following Him on white horses. And from His mouth comes a sharp sword, so that with it He may smite the nations; and He will rule them with a rod of iron; and he treads the wine press of the fierce wrath of God, the Almighty. And on His robe and on His thigh He has a name written, "KING OF KINGS, AND LORD OF LORDS."

This is the culminating event of human history and has been anticipated throughout the prophetic portions of Scripture.

In Isaiah 63:3, Christ's coming in wrath is described as Him treading the wine trough in anger, "and their lifeblood is sprinkled on My garments and I stained all My raiment."

In Zechariah 14:3-4 it was prophesied, "The LORD will go forth and fight against those nations, as when He fights on a day of battle. And in that day His feet will stand on the Mount of Olives, which is in front of Jerusalem on the east; and the Mount of Olives will be split in its middle from east to west by a very large valley, so that half of the mountain will move toward the north and the other half toward the south." The Mount of Olives was Christ's point of departure when He left the disciples (Acts 1:9), so apparently it will be His point of return. Indeed, the angel had told the amazed disciples, "This Jesus, who has been taken up from you into heaven, will come in just the same way as you have watched Him go into heaven" (Acts 1:11). Psalm 2:1-9 prophesies His return very specifically as it speaks of God's Son inheriting the nations whom He shall break with a rod of iron—the same terminology used in Revelation 19:15.

The familiar passage in Isaiah 9:6-7 predicts both of His advents:

> For a child will be born to us, a son will be given to us; and the government will rest on His shoulders; and His name will be called Wonderful Counselor, Mighty God, Eternal Father, Prince of Peace. There will be no end to the increase of His government or of peace, on the throne of David and over His kingdom, to establish it and to uphold it with justice and righteousness from then on forevermore.

Christ Himself described His return in Matthew 24:27-51, including a description of society at the time of His arrival. A brief selection of verses from that passage provides a summary of Christ's comments:

> "But immediately after the tribulation of those days THE SUN WILL BE DARKENED, AND THE MOON WILL NOT GIVE ITS LIGHT, AND THE STARS WILL FALL from the sky, and the powers of the heavens will be shaken, and then the sign of the Son of Man will appear in the sky, and then all the tribes of the earth will mourn, and they will see the SON OF MAN COMING ON THE CLOUDS OF THE SKY with power and great glory."
> —Matthew 24:29-30

> "Even so you too, when you see all these things, recognize that He is near, right at the door. Truly I say to you, this generation will not pass away until all these things take place…But of that day and hour no one knows, not even the angels of heaven, nor the Son, but the Father alone. For the coming of the Son of Man will be just like the days of Noah…"
> —Matthew 24:33-37

"Therefore be on the alert, for you do not know which day your Lord is coming."

—Matthew 24:42

"For this reason you be ready too; for the Son of Man is coming at an hour when you do not think He will."

—Matthew 24:44

His eyes and mouth are described in verses 12 and 15 just as they were in Revelation 1—His eyes are a flame of fire (see also 1:14) and "from His mouth comes a sharp sword, so that with it He may smite the nations; and He will rule them with a rod of iron" (see also 1:16). In chapter 1 the sword had two edges, for the word proceeding from His mouth could cut either way, to bless or destroy. His purpose in chapter 19 is to express His wrath and destroy the armies of the beast; therefore, the sword needs only one edge. After the completion of His victorious second coming, He will rule the nations with a rod of iron. Some commentators have opined that only the righteous will have a part in this kingdom. Apparently, however, sin will still be active in the world even though Satan will be imprisoned for a thousand years. Christ would not have to rule with a "rod of iron" if it were not so. (More on that in the commentary on chapter 20.)

The armies of heaven follow Him. They are dressed in fine linen, white and clean. Recall that in 17:14, those who wage war on the side of the Lamb "are the called and chosen and faithful." If the clothing and the three terms are identifiers, it would seem that any one or all of the three groups of the church, the Jews, and the tribulation saints follow Christ into battle. In Matthew 24:31, as He describes His second coming, Christ says He will send forth His angels with a great trumpet, so angels may also be in His entourage but are not included in the called, chosen, and faithful group. Whoever may be in Christ's army, they are certainly not there as support troops. He doesn't need them to fight the battle; He must only speak to destroy, and He does. Verse 20 indicates that after the beast and the false prophet are seized, the rest will be killed with the sword that comes from His mouth.

Verses 17-21

John sees the results of Christ's return to earth beginning with an angel standing in the sun crying out in anticipation of the slaughter that is about to happen, saying to all the birds that fly in mid-heaven, "Come, assemble for the great supper of God." The angel proceeds to describe that supper as being the flesh of men and horses in the army of the beast who will be killed with the sword that comes from the mouth of Him who sat upon the white horse. The beast, who led the army of the kings of the earth against Christ and His army, is seized. With him is also seized the false prophet whose signs had deceived those who received the mark of the beast and who worshiped his image. These two are thrown alive into the lake of fire which burns with brimstone.

The army of the beast that is destroyed by Christ's return was mentioned in 16:13-16. In that passage, three demons had gone out to the kings of the whole world to gather them together to the place which in Hebrew is called Har-Magedon. We know it as Armageddon. Some believe that Ezekiel 37–39 describes this battle, primarily due to 39:17-20 that parallels Revelation 19:17-18, describing the slaughter as providing food for the birds. I believe that the event in Ezekiel is related to another time, which I will discuss in comments on chapter 20.

Chapter 16 indicates that the demons went out to the kings of the "whole world" (16:14). If the whole earth as we know it today is considered, and all the kings or leaders are thought to be included in the army of the beast, there would be literally hundreds of nations represented. There would then appear to be a discrepancy between this passage and several other passages in Scripture that have been considered.

For example, Daniel 2:40-45 describes a stone cut without hands that strikes the feet and ten toes of Nebuchadnezzar's statue, destroying it. The ten toes had been described as those kings arising from the fourth and final kingdom. In Daniel 7, the vision is of a kingdom consisting of ten kings described as ten horns that are brought down by the court that sits for judgment (Daniel 7:26). In Revelation chapters 13 and 17, reference is made to the seven heads and ten horns of Satan and the final beast. In each case the ten horns are identified as kingdoms that are under control of the antichrist. So there are several references to the kingdoms that the Lord destroys at the end of time, and in each reference they are ten in number. It would appear, therefore, that the battle described in Revelation 19 is the battle of Armageddon. The armies that are involved are those of the ten kings and not those of the whole earth as we know it today. See the commentary on 16:13-14 for a discussion of the world of that time as defined by Herbert Lockyer's *Illustrated Dictionary of the Bible.*

The beast and the false prophet are thrown alive into the lake of fire, which apparently is hell. They seem to be the first two residents as no other Scripture comments on anyone being disposed of there until these two are captured. After these two are seized, the rest of their army is killed by the sword proceeding from the mouth of Him who sits on the white horse. As mentioned above, He did not need the army that went with Him for military support, but may have it to display His glory and power.

REVELATION 20

The end of chapter 19 saw the doom of the beast (the antichrist) and his false prophet. Both were "thrown alive into the lake of fire which burns with brimstone" (19:20). Here in chapter 20, The attention is directed to the third and main character of the evil threesome—Satan himself.

Verses 1-3

John sees an angel coming from heaven with the key to the abyss and a great chain in his hand. The angel "laid hold of the dragon, the serpent of old, who is the devil and Satan, and bound him for a thousand years; and threw him into the abyss, and shut it and sealed it over him."

There are several interesting matters in this passage. First is the matter of the key. There seem to be several keys to the abyss, or one key that is being passed around among various parties. In 9:1-2, a star fell from heaven and was referred to as "he"; we interpreted that star to be Satan or one of his angel-demons that fell from heaven. He was given the key to the bottomless pit, which he then used to open the pit and release destroying locusts. In 20:1, the key to the abyss is in the hands of an angel from heaven, which he uses to open the abyss and throw Satan into it. We are, of course, assuming that the bottomless pit in chapter 9 and the abyss in chapter 20 are the same location. This pit is most certainly not Hades (Greek for hell) because Christ holds that key (1:18).

Satan is not disposed of in the lake of fire at this time, as were the other two; instead, he is thrown into the abyss and "must be released for a short time" after a thousand years. That this angel is able to bind Satan with such apparent ease causes us to wonder if it is Christ Himself, particularly in view of the tentativeness with which Michael, the archangel, treated Satan in Jude 9. Most commentators do not believe that it is Christ.

The method of binding—with a chain—seems to be rather improbable considering Satan's power and his being a spirit. However, if not a literal chain, then the word chain refers to something, even a Word spoken by God, that will hold Satan in confinement for a thousand years. And, of course, it is a surprise that Satan will be released again, but we are not told why this is allowed by God.

Verses 4-5

John observes thrones. The power to judge was given to those who sat on the thrones. John then sees the souls of those "beheaded because of the testimony of Jesus and because of the word of God, and those who had not worshiped the beast or his image, and had not received the mark upon their forehead and upon their hand; and they came to life and reigned with Christ for a thousand years. The rest of the dead did not come to life until the thousand years were completed. This is the first resurrection."

Here, again, John sees what I believe to be the court of twenty-four elders, for they are the only ones (besides God Himself) who have been described as sitting on thrones (4:4; 11:16). John emphasizes that they have the power to judge, and this disclosure is immediately followed by John's observation of a resurrection of the tribulation saints. This group consisted of those who had been beheaded because of their testimony of Jesus and because of the word of God and those who had been victorious over the beast. Those victorious over the beast had already been presented standing on the sea of glass (15:2) where the thrones of the twenty-four elders had been set up (4:4-6). These souls had probably just testified against the evil threesome and, as pointed out in 12:11, "They overcame him [Satan] because of the blood of the Lamb and because of the word of their testimony." As noted in the chapter 13 commentary, it is very likely that the mark of the beast was instituted in Israel so most of these martyrs are Jews and may be Christian for they sang the song of Moses and the song of the Lamb (15:3). It is probable that since they are going with Jesus as He goes to reign for a thousand years on David's throne as King of the Jews, that they would all be Jewish in order to participate in His administration over Israel, for the "time of the Gentiles" has come to an end.

John sees the souls of those who had been beheaded; he does not see their bodies without heads, so must have been told that they were beheaded. The beheading of those who opposed the antichrist seems to be the principal way of disposing of disobedient people during the time of the tribulation; however, that term may be used in a generic way by John, to describe any of those killed. Only in recent months have Westerners seen the horror of beheadings for this seems to be the preferred method that insurgent Muslims choose to kill their prisoners.

The judgments against the beast, the false prophet, and Satan himself have been rendered by the twenty-four elders, and the sentences executed. The souls of the tribulation saints are now joined with their resurrection bodies to be priests of God and Christ and to reign with Him on earth for a thousand years.

Verse 5 states that the rest of the dead will not be resurrected until the thousand-year reign of Christ is completed. These resurrections were probably those spoken of in Daniel 12:2, "Many of those who sleep in the dust of the ground will awake, these to everlasting life, but the others to disgrace and everlasting contempt." Daniel was speaking of and to Jews, so I expect many of the tribulation saints seen by John in the Revelation passage are Jews. "This is the first resurrection." Verse 6 provides the fifth beatitude of Revelation: "Blessed and holy is the one who has a part in the first resurrection," indicating that those who participate in the first resurrection will not be concerned with the second death and will reign with Christ a thousand years.

There has been great discussion and differences of opinion among students and commentators of Revelation regarding the term "first resurrection." It cannot be truly the "first" as there are several instances in Scripture, prior to this time, when people came out of the grave—including Christ's own resurrection and the rapture of the church when "the Lord Himself will descend from heaven…and the dead in Christ shall rise first" (1 Thessalonians 4:16). The word *first* is probably used here to designate between those who are raised from the dead because of their faith (for which they were killed during the tribulation), and those who are raised a thousand years later. It is presumed that the later resurrection (note that it is *not* called the "second" resurrection) consists of those included in the great white throne judgment, described in verses 11-15 and discussed below.

Verse 6

What about this thousand-year reign of Christ? What information does Scripture provide about those days? Revelation 19:15 describes that when Christ returns, He will rule the nations "with a rod of iron." Psalm 2 describes the distress of the nations that, during the millennium, want to tear loose the fetters with which they feel the Lord has them bound. The Lord's response is to laugh and tell them that they are given to His Son who will "break them with a rod of iron" (Psalm 2:9). This tells us that after Christ returns and Satan is bound, Christ will have to rule the nations with a rod of iron due to their rebellious nature and the continued prevalence of sin even though Satan is imprisoned.

Other Scriptures tell us that Christ will reestablish the throne of David and His reign will never end. This fulfills the covenant God made with David: "Your house and your kingdom shall endure before Me forever; your throne shall be established forever" (2 Samuel 7:16). Isaiah 9:7 says, "There will be no end to the increase of His government or of peace, on the throne of David and over his kingdom, to establish it and to uphold it with justice and righteousness from then on and forevermore." In Luke 1:32-33 the angel announced to Mary, "The Lord God will give Him the throne of His father David; and He will reign over the house of Jacob forever; and His kingdom will have no end." In His first advent He came as a servant and not as a king (that being one of the reasons the Jews did not recognize Him as their Messiah). At His second coming, He will take the throne of David and reign forever.

During the millennium, however, His rule is only over the nation of Israel (David's throne), so how does He control the other nations of the world? Apparently, His "rod of iron" includes blessings on Israel and the nations that serve Israel, judgment on nations that do not. Isaiah 60:1–63:6 which gives a general description of the millennium, shows how the nation of Israel becomes respected among the nations, and provides an idea of the control Christ will exercise: "Your gates will be open continually; they will not be closed day or night, so that men may bring to you the wealth of the nations, with their kings led in procession. For the nation and the kingdom which will not serve you will perish, and the nations will be utterly ruined" (Isaiah 60:11-12). Isaiah 2:2 describes how Israel will be treated during the millennium, "Now it will come about that in the last days, the mountain [kingdom] of the house of the LORD will be established as the chief of the mountains, and will be raised above the hills; and all the nations will stream to it." Verse 3 continues the description, commenting that people want to go to the mountain of the Lord to learn His way and walk in His paths, and it states that "the law will go forth from Zion [Jerusalem]." A few selected comments from a familiar passage, Isaiah 11:1-10, also describe the rule of Christ: The Spirit of the Lord will be on Him; He will judge the poor with righteousness; with the rod of His mouth He will rule the earth and slay the wicked; wild animals will be at peace with domestic animals and a little boy shall lead them; the earth will be full of the knowledge of the Lord; the nations will come to Jesus as Lord and Ruler. So, with Christ on David's throne during the millennium, Israel becomes the new super power.

There will probably be a repopulation of the earth during this time after the tribulation and the vast percentages of the earth's people who had been raptured or killed. According to Isaiah 65, death will still be existent, but life will be of longer duration during the millennium. Isaiah 65:20 indicates that anyone not living to at least a hundred years old will be thought to be accursed. Looking back a thousand years in history and considering how the population has grown despite wars, famine, and disease, I believe we can expect an even greater increase during Christ's reign of peace—longer life and presumably continued advancements in medicine and technology.

Verses 7-10

After being restricted for a thousand years, Satan will be released (he "must be released for a short time," according to verse 3). Satan cannot change. The moment of his release he begins the battle which he has apparently been planning for those thousand years. Oddly enough, he is immediately able to raise a large army. Even though "the earth will be full of the knowledge of the LORD" (Isaiah 11:9) during the millennium, there will still be a large contingent of unsaved people willing to rebel against the millennial government of Christ. There must also, then, be a large contingent of people who were saved, some of whom are still alive and others who have died. Scripture does not address their future as it did those of the church age and those of the tribulation age. They are not part of the church that was raptured, they are not part of the tribulation saints that reign with Christ, nor are they mentioned as part of the great white throne judgment.

There are various theories and speculations regarding the millennial reign of Christ and the final release of Satan. Some do not believe that the reference to a thousand years is literal but is merely descriptive of a substantial period of time. Some believe that the binding of Satan is happening now, that Christ is currently reigning from heaven, and that we are currently in the millennium. Some even say that this event is impossible of literal fulfillment. There are rebuttals to each of these concerns, however, suffice it to say that I, again, believe that the literal interpretation is the most acceptable and logical, and that this refers to a literal one-thousand-year period after Christ's return.

There are also various thoughts as to why Satan is to be released after a thousand years. These have to do with proving to man how weak and immoral his character is, and how, even under ideal conditions, he is rebellious to the core. He cannot live a sinless life and needs Christ's sacrifice to rescue him from eternal damnation. Eventual eternal punishment is therefore justified. Scripture does not give us much information regarding either the millennium or the release of Satan, so it can only be said that they are a couple of mysteries that cannot be resolved from what the Lord has provided. It does seem, however, that during the millennium most conditions on earth—such as governments, personal relationships, economics—are much the same as before Christ's return.

Religious exercise, with Christ being the focal point, and Israel's position as the world power will be the key differences.

After Satan is released from his thousand-year imprisonment, he "will come out to deceive the nations which are in the four corners of the earth, Gog and Magog, to gather them together for the war." Apparently the "four corners" description indicates that all the nations of the world will be deceived. The representatives of these nations, presumably their armies, will surround "the camp of the saints and the beloved city." The camp of the saints may be a settlement outside Jerusalem for those who came with Christ to be part of His millennial reign (20:4). It is reasonably certain that the beloved city is Jerusalem.

Scripture describes a quick and decisive end to the rebels in one verse. They are devoured by fire from heaven. The devil himself is unceremoniously "thrown into the lake of fire and brimstone, where the beast and the false prophet are also; and they will be tormented day and night forever and ever." This verse confirms that the spirit never dies. The beast and false prophet have already been in this lake for a thousand years, and they will continue to be tormented forever.

A LOOK AT EZEKIEL 37, 38, AND 39

Gog and Magog are the names used in Revelation 20:8 to describe the nations in the "four corners of the earth" that Satan will deceive and gather together for war. These are familiar names from Ezekiel, but are they the same entities spoken of in Ezekiel 38:2? There it states, "Son of man, set your face toward Gog of the land of Magog, the prince of Rosh, Meshech, and Tubal." If they are not, where does the war spoken of in Ezekiel 38 and 39 fall into the end time events?

It appears from the Ezekiel text that Gog must be a prince of the three cities that are located in a land or country called Magog. There are several thoughts on this from commentators. Some believe that Russia is indicated by the words Rosh, Meshech, and Tubal, which they translate into Russia, Moscow, and Tobolsk. In addition 38:15 and 39:2 speak of this invader coming from the remote part of the north, which has been thought to refer to Russia. According to Ezekiel 38:5-6, these three are joined by Persia, Ethiopia, Put, Gomer, and Beth-torgamah, which, except for the last two, are familiar nations. (It is fairly certain that Put is Lybia.) Some believe the last two refer to Germany, but that is speculation. Some believe this invasion, headed by Russia, is to occur sometime during the first three-and-a-half years of the tribulation, and may be the incursion from the north spoken of in Daniel 11:44. Others hold to the Russian theory, but believe that it occurs during the early years of the millennium. To others it is not about Russia but is a description of the battle of Armageddon due to the similarity of the description of the feast for the birds in Ezekiel 39:4 and 39:17-20 and in Revelation 19:17-18.

The participants, Gomer, Magog, Meshech, and Tubal, are listed in Genesis 10:2 as sons born after the flood to Japheth, one of Noah's three sons. Put is a son of Ham, another of Noah's sons (Genesis 10:6). Rosh appears as the son of Benjamin in Genesis 46:21 and has no apparent connection with the establishment of nations. According to the Table of Nations from the *International Standard Bible Encyclopedia*, there were seventy nations established by Noah's three sons. These sons and their families settled the southern and eastern shores of the Black Sea, as well as Egypt and northern Africa. According to the *Atlas of the Bible Lands* published by Scripture Press, Meshech, Tubal, and Gomer were in what is now Turkey. Magog was in the area between the Black Sea and the Caspian Sea, which had, for many years, been the southern part of Russia. Those countries that have recently broken with Russia—Georgia, Armenia, Azerbaijan, Uzbekistan, and several others—have now become independent states. Specifically, the nations thought to be descended from those four grandsons of Noah, mentioned in Ezekiel, are as follows:

Magog—Greeks, Romans, French, Italian, Spanish
Tubal—The peoples south of the Black Sea
Meshech—Russians
Gomer—Celtic peoples

The purpose in exploring the Genesis genealogy of Noah's sons and the nations that are thought to have descended from them is to dispel the idea that these names in themselves are descriptive of present-day cities or nations. They may, however, point to certain nations. Ezekiel's world was very narrow and there would have been no thoughts of Russia, and even Rome or Greece were of very little consequence in Ezekiel's time, about 600 B.C. He was, however, aware of the settlements far to the north around the Black Sea, for in 38:6 he referred to "Beth-togarmah from the remote parts of the north." According to footnotes in Zondervan's NASB translation, Torgarmah was Gomer's son and he settled in the area which today is Armenia, one of those countries that recently broke off from Russia, Armenia has had an ongoing feud with Turkey over land taken by Turkey and many Armenians have been killed by the Turks.

I believe that it was probably those countries around the Black Sea to which Ezekiel referred to being from the far north. There is certainly reason to suspect Russia's involvement since they are considered to be established by descendants of Meshech. Another reason that some commentators consider Russia to be the leader is based upon the relationship of the sons of Japheth and the nations mentioned above. Those nations were located in the south of Russia and were part of the Russian Federation until the Federation broke up in 1991.

Ezekiel's reference to the "remote parts of the north" probably only extended to the Black Sea and referred to those nations that were either first established in the area which is now Turkey, or those nations that broke with Russia—all of which are of the Islamic faith. Also, as mentioned earlier, the attitude of the nations toward Israel leads to the conclusion that the Islamic nations are the primary enemies of Israel and would be the most likely nations to attack Israel. Although Russia or any of the European countries may decide to intervene on behalf of an Arab nation, they have not the real desire to eliminate Israel from the face of the earth as do the Islamic nations.

As to the timing of this invasion, I believe there are enough clues in place to establish a pretty good guess. Ezekiel 37 includes two significant items. First is the well-known prophecy of the valley of dry bones. The Lord raises the "whole house of Israel" (37:11) out of their graves (nations where they are in exile), breathes life into them, and brings them into the land of Israel and unites Ephraim (Israel) and Judah into one nation. This prophecy is, at least, partially fulfilled at the present time as many Jews have returned to Israel. But there are still many scattered among the nations of the world.

The invasion described in chapter 38 must, therefore, occur after the Jewish people are back in Israel. The second indicator is the promise in 37:24, "My servant David will be king over them, and they will all have one shepherd; and they will walk in My ordinances, and keep My statutes, and observe them." This indicates that David's kingdom will have been restored. Some interpret this scripture to mean that David will be resurrected and returned to his throne. There are several references to the filling of David's throne, none indicating that David himself will be resurrected. One of these references is Isaiah 9:6, "For a child will be born to us" followed in verse 7 by the words, "There will be no end to the increase of His government or of peace, on the throne of David and over his kingdom." The other reference is Luke 1:32 where the angel announced to Mary that she will bear Jesus, "The Lord God will give Him the throne of His father David." From these and other scriptures, the Jewish people thought that one evidence of the Messiah, when He appeared, would be that He would take David's throne. Since Christ was not in view in Ezekiel's day, and obviously was not to be revealed, God spoke to Ezekiel about His servant David, which must have been a real mystery to Ezekiel. Christ is, however, the only promised successor to David's throne, so it has to be Christ about whom scripture was speaking when Ezekiel wrote in 37:24, "My servant David will be king over them."

Considering that the only time Christ will reign on earth will be during the millennium, then it must be at that time that He will sit on David's throne. That indicates then, that this attack on Israel, described in Ezekiel 38 and 39 must take place during the millennium.

Most commentators do not consider the Ezekiel battle to be the same one described in Revelation 20:8-9 at the end of the millennium after Satan has been released. There are several reasons, one being the seven-year cleanup described in Ezekiel 39:9. The defeat of Satan is followed immediately, in the latter part of Revelation 20, with the description of the great white throne judgment. It does not appear there will be a period of seven years in which to conduct a cleanup, but this is speculation since there is no indication that the judgment must immediately follow the destruction of Satan and his army. It is certainly possible that the great white throne judgment will be some time later.

Another differentiation is that Gog seems to be referring to a nation in Revelation; however, in Ezekiel it refers to Gog as a prince. The Revelation reference is, however, somewhat obscure.

The indication in Revelation 20 is that Satan will deceive the nations, Gog and Magog, and gather them together for the war and "the number of them is like the sand of the seashore." When it speaks of numbers being like the sand of the seashore (20:8), it does not seem that the nations involved would be that numerous, so it is probably speaking of the size of the armies. Consequently, only a few nations may be involved, similar to those noted in Ezekiel 38. Since Gog and Magog are used only once before in Scripture, in Ezekiel 38, it seems that the reference to them here would be an indication by the Holy Spirit that the same group of people is going to be raised one more time against His chosen ones. From the position of Gog and Magog in the middle of the verse, it also seems that they could be referring to both nations and leaders, just as they were in Ezekiel. Other indicators of the timing of the invasion of Israel in Ezekiel 38–39 are:

1. Inhabitants (Jews) have been gathered from many nations to Israel and are living securely (38:8).
2. The people will be living without walls (38:11).
3. It will come about "in the last days" (38:16).
4. Gog was spoken of in former days, through the prophets, that he would be brought against God's people Israel in order that the nations may know Him (38:16-17).
5. There will be a great earthquake in land of Israel (38:19).
6. Mountains will be thrown down and walls will collapse (38:20).
7. Internal conflict will arise in the army of the attackers (38:21).
8. God will judge Gog with pestilence, rain with hailstones, fire, and brimstone (38:22).
9. Gog will fall on the mountains of Israel and become food for birds and animals (39:4-5).
10. God will send fire on Magog and the coastlands (39:6).
11. The nations will know that God is the Lord of Israel and they will not profane His holy name anymore (39:7).

12. Israelites will burn the weapons of Gog, making fires that will last for seven years (39:9).
13. Gog will be buried in Israel, in the valley of Hamon-gog (39:11).
14. Israelites will bury the dead of Gog for seven months (39:12).
15. Birds and beasts will be called to eat the flesh and drink the blood of all those killed (39:17-19).
16. God shall set His glory among the nations and Israel will know that He is the Lord their God (39:21-22).

Revelation informs us of only two conflicts during the millennium—at Christ's return when He throws the antichrist and the false prophet into the lake of fire at the battle of Armageddon (19:20), and the final defeat of Satan when he too is thrown into the lake of fire at the end of the millennium (20:10).

Several of the above signs indicate that the Ezekiel 38–39 battle coincides with the battle against Satan at the end of the thousand years.

From Ezekiel 37:21 we know that the Jews have been recalled to Israel; this is also confirmed in Ezekiel 38:8 (see Item 1 above). In Ezekiel 37:24, God says to Ezekiel, "My servant David will be king over them," a reference to David's throne and, as discussed earlier, is indication that Christ is sitting on that throne. Therefore, the battle would be at some time after Christ has reestablished David's throne. That can only be during the millennium.

Ezekiel 38:11 (Item 2 above) indicates that the Jews are living in peace, which they would not be at the time of Christ's second advent but certainly would be at the end of His thousand-year reign.

Items 5, 6, 7, 8, and 10 all indicate that God is the one who inflicts judgment on and destroys the army of Gog, which He does in the defeat of Satan and his armies in both of the conflicts in Revelation. If the Gog of Ezekiel and the one in Revelation are the same entity, and if Ezekiel and Revelation describe two different battles (conducted by the one Gog), the one in Revelation would have to precede the one in Ezekiel since Gog is said to be buried in Israel after the battle in Ezekiel (Item 13 above) Another possibility is that the Ezekiel battle is not reported in Revelation, but this does not seem likely. Since the Ezekiel invasion is most certainly at some time during the millennium, due to the various indications discussed above, it is my opinion that the Ezekiel battle is a description of the one at the end of the millennium described in Revelation 20, when Satan is thrown into the lake of fire.

RETURN TO REVELATION 20

Verse 11

John sees a great white throne and One sitting on it from whose very presence heaven and earth fled from view and John says, "No place was found for them." This could well be the time spoken of in Hebrews 1:10-11, "THOU, LORD, IN THE BEGINNING DIDST LAY THE FOUNDATION OF THE EARTH, AND THE HEAVENS ARE THE WORKS OF THY HANDS; THEY WILL PERISH, BUT THOU REMAINEST; AND THEY ALL WILL BECOME OLD AS A GARMENT, AND AS A MANTLE THOU WILT ROLL THEM UP; AS A GARMENT THEY WILL ALSO BE CHANGED." And in 2 Peter 3:10, "But the day of the Lord will come like a thief, in which the heavens will pass away with a roar and the elements will be destroyed with intense heat, and the earth and its works will be burned up." We are not told that this is the time of the destruction of earth and heaven, but just four verses after they disappear from view (as chapter 21 begins), John sees a new heaven and a new earth.

Verses 12-15

The resurrection of the rest of the dead, promised in verse 5 to occur after the thousand years are completed, now comes to pass. John describes the subjects he sees and their judgments. The dead, great and small, stand before the throne and the books (plural) are opened, and then another book is opened which is the book of life. The other books must be records of deeds done on earth, for John indicates the people are judged according to their deeds that are written in the books.

John then tells us that the sea and death and Hades give up their dead for judgment. We can only guess at what is meant by this, but it seems that the implication of including the sea, death, and Hades is that everyone who is dead who had not otherwise been resurrected will be raised, no matter what the condition of the body nor where it is located.

After everyone is judged, then all evil will be consolidated in the lake of fire: Death, Hades, and all those whose names are not in the book of life are thrown into the lake of fire. The lake of fire is the second death, and the last enemy to be abolished is death (1 Corinthians 15:26)

This judgment leaves us with a mystery. Many believe the great white throne judgment is only of the wicked dead. Daniel 12:2, John 5:29, and Acts 24:15 all speak of the resurrection of the righteous and the wicked as if there will be two resurrections, but none of them declare specifically that there will be two resurrections. Revelation 20:4-5 does speak of two resurrections, the first being those who had been faithful during the tribulation and the rest of the dead one thousand years later. Scripture does not tell us that the second one was of the wicked only. I believe the second one includes all of the unsaved dead from the days of Adam to the end of the millennium, but if that is all that it includes then there are groups not accounted for.

We have only scraps of information in Scripture regarding the final disposition of those who are saved and those who are unsaved during the various windows of time. The following is a summary of the time periods and certain verses relative to those coming out of each time period. This is not an exhaustive analysis, but sufficient for the purpose of drawing certain conclusions.

Time Period: From the time of creation to the advent of Christ:	
Righteous—Alive	None
Righteous—Dead	Abraham's bosom (Luke 16:19-31). There are no Gentiles that we know of who are saved during this time period for the Lord worked only among His chosen people, the Jews. They went to Abraham's bosom at death which is probably located in heaven or paradise. We know John saw two groups, one under the altar in Revelation 6:9, which I believe to be Jews, and another group standing before the throne in 7:9, which I believe are Christians. The two groups that John saw are apparently in the same area (heaven or paradise) but in separate locations.
Unrighteous—Alive	None
Unrighteous—Dead	Hades (Luke 16:19-31), awaiting the great white throne judgment of Revelation 20:11.

Time Period: From Christ's crucifixion until the rapture—the church age	
Righteous—Alive	None
Saved—Alive	Raptured (1 Thessalonians 4:16-17). The dead in Christ shall rise first. Then those who are alive and remain shall be caught up together with them in the clouds to meet the Lord in the air. These are both Gentiles and Jews who have believed in Christ and His sacrifice for the sins of the world in His death, burial, and resurrection (John 3:16-18).
Saved—Dead	See above.
Unsaved—Alive	Go into the tribulation period.
Unsaved—Dead	Hades (Luke 16:19-31), awaiting the great white throne judgment of Revelation 20:11.

Time Period: Seven-year tribulation period.	
Saved—Alive	The saved who are alive at the end of the tribulation are not specifically discussed in Scripture, but would undoubtedly go into the millennium.
Saved—Dead	There is a great multitude standing before the throne that came out of the great tribulation. They are assigned to serve God day and night in His temple (Revelation 7:9-15). There is another group that John sees under the altar who, as discussed in chapter 6, I believe are Jews (Revelation 6:9-10). There is no indication that they came out of the tribulation; however, their attitude toward those on earth, who are in the tribulation period, would indicate that some, if not all, came out of the tribulation. We are not told where the people in this group are destined to go, but they are in heaven rejoicing over the destruction of Babylon (Revelation 19:1-13). There is another group that may be part of those under the altar, for I believe they are Jews. These are those who were beheaded for the testimony of Jesus and for not worshiping the beast and his image. They will reign with Christ for a thousand years (Revelation 20:4). That they are going to reign with Jesus would imply that they are Jewish for He is going to occupy the throne of David and take His position as King of the Jews. I would think those reigning with Him would be Jews.
Unsaved—Alive	Go into the millennium.
Unsaved—Dead	Hades (Luke 16:19-31), awaiting the great white throne judgment of Revelation 20:11.

Time Period: Millennium—Thousand-year reign of Christ.	
Saved—Alive	The earth will be full of the knowledge of the Lord (Isaiah 11:9). This verse is in a passage thought to be a brief description of life during the millennium. If this passage is applicable to the millennium, then it sounds as if there would be people saved. Those who are saved would go directly into the eternal Kingdom according to Matthew 13:41-43.
Saved—Dead	We are not told the disposition of this group. It is possible that they would be in the group of dead that are included in the great white throne judgment.
Unsaved—Alive	According to Christ's parables in Matthew 13:41-43, 49-50, at the end of the age angels will separate the wicked from the righteous and throw them into the furnace of fire.
Unsaved—Dead	The dead, including those of Satan's army who are destroyed by fire at the final battle after the millennium, will be included in the great white throne judgment.

Time Period: Great white throne judgment

Following the millennium, John observed the great white throne and the dead who were standing before the throne. That they are all of the dead who had not otherwise been resurrected is implied by the places that gave up their dead—the sea and death and Hades (Hades would include all of those unsaved from all time periods noted above). Those standing before the throne were judged based upon their deeds as recorded in the books. This is emphasized, for it is repeated in Revelation 20:12-13, so the judgment must have been based upon God's law and not on Christ and His fulfillment of that law. The dead may include the righteous from the millennium. They are not referred to elsewhere, and there seems to be an implication that some among the dead were included in the book of life. The last comment before leaving the judgment seat is "and if anyone's name was not found written in the book of life, he was thrown into the lake of fire" (20:15). If all were going to the lake of fire, it does not seem that this last comment would be necessary.

REVELATION 21

Verse 1

As chapter 21 opens, John sees a new heaven and a new earth for the first heaven and first earth passed away, and there is no longer any sea. It is assumed that the first heaven and earth passed away as the great white throne judgment was beginning in 20:11. There are two items of interest as this takes place. The first is the realization that the lake of fire must not be associated with the earth, as many assume. Scripture does not provide any information as to where the lake of fire or hell is, but if the old earth is to be destroyed and replaced, it certainly is not a part of our present earth.

The second is the comment that there is no longer any sea. This seems to indicate that water to sustain life will no longer be provided by the atmosphere. In our present state, all living things, whether plant or animal, require water to live. We live in a water world, as Peter expressed it in 2 Peter 3:5, "By the word of God the heavens existed long ago and the earth was formed out of water and by water." This may have been the basis of Christ's reference when answering Nicodemus's question regarding how to be born again. He said in John 3:5, "Unless one is born of water and the Spirit, he cannot enter into the kingdom of God." In other words, it was only this water world that Christ came to save, and you had to be of this world and a believer in His sacrifice on the cross. Those of the spiritual world—angels, for instance—are not candidates for being born of the Holy Spirit. In the new earth, it appears that there will be only one source of water—a river of the water of life coming from the throne of God. If water is needed to sustain life in plants and animals (I believe that we will have both in heaven, but that's another subject) as well as humans, it appears that this river will be the source.

We are told nothing more of the new heaven and the new earth in Revelation and must go back to the Old Testament for a small amount of additional information. God said to Isaiah in 65:17-18 that He will create "new heavens and a new earth" and create Jerusalem for rejoicing and her people for gladness. In the New Testament, in 2 Peter 3:13, Peter says, "But according to His promise we are looking for new heavens and a new earth, in which righteousness dwells."

Verses 2-4

John then sees "the holy city, new Jerusalem, coming down out of heaven from God, made ready as a bride." And he hears a loud voice announcing, "Behold, the tabernacle of God is among men, and He shall dwell among them." In verse 4 the announcement continues that "He shall wipe away every tear from their eyes; and there shall no longer be any death; there shall no longer be any mourning, or crying, or pain; the first things have passed away." This is somewhat explained in the passage in Isaiah 65, referred to above. In that passage, after the reference to the new heavens and new earth God says, "And the former things shall not be remembered or come to mind" (Isaiah 65:17). Apparently we will no longer remember the old earth, the pain and suffering there, nor those loved ones who did not make it to heaven. In the lack of memory there will be no more tears.

We often hear it said that there will be no more tears when we get to heaven. It does seem, however, that according to Christ's story of the rich man and Lazarus in Luke 16:19-31, we shall still be quite aware and concerned about our loved ones who are still alive. Certainly those folks under the altar in Revelation 6:9-10 remembered their treatment on earth and wanted revenge. In Revelation 7:17, one of the elders told John that God *shall* (a future action) wipe away the tears from the eyes of those who were in the multitude standing before the throne and the Lamb. Scripture does not indicate that our tears will be no more until the end of the millennium when the new heaven and earth are created and we enter the eternal state. At that time there will also be a cessation of death, mourning, crying, and pain. These things have passed away and we are in the presence of God who has created all things new, and whose dwelling place will be among men.

Verses 5-8

"He who sits on the throne said, 'Behold, I am making all things new.'" John, who is probably so engrossed that he has to be reminded of what he is there for, is told to "write, for these words are faithful and true."

The One on the throne then says to John, "It is done. I am the Alpha and the Omega, the beginning and the end," and by these words identifies Himself as Christ, for that is the way He was introduced in 1:8 as Revelation opened. He indicates that His promise made in John 14:2 that "I go to prepare a place for you," has been completed. He has delivered up the kingdom to God the Father in accord with 1 Corinthians 15:24, with the words "It is done," much as He had indicated that the first phase was completed on the cross with the words, "It is finished!" (John 19:30).

Just as it was promised to those who were martyred during the great tribulation that the Lamb would guide them to springs of the water of life (7:17), so Christ reaffirms that promise here: To anyone who thirsts He will give to them from the spring of the water of life. This spring is probably the river of the water of life described as coming from under the throne of God and the Lamb in 22:1. This may refer to the abundant life available in the new heaven and earth, much like what must have been intended by God as He first created Adam and Eve in the Garden. This seems to be confirmed as He says in verse 7, "He who overcomes shall inherit these things, and I will be his God and he will be My son." The "things" to be inherited are not mentioned, but can only refer to the new life as described—without death, tears, or pain—life that will truly be abundant" (John 10:10). These overcomers will be treated as sons of the Creator of the universe. These promises must be directed to those believers who are not part of the church, for the church is the bride of Christ and would not be considered as a son (see verse 9).

Diametrically opposite this wonderful existence will be the existence of "the cowardly and unbelieving and abominable and murderers and immoral persons and sorcerers and idolaters and all liars, their part will be in the lake that burns with fire and brimstone, which is the second death." As discussed above, this sounds like the interior of our present earth, but we know that the earth has been destroyed. Wherever it is, this lake is separated from God and is not the place to spend eternity.

Verses 9-17

The next scene is introduced to John by one of the seven angels who had the seven bowls full of the seven last plagues. He says to John, "Come here, I shall show you the bride, the wife of the Lamb." With that, they go to a high place and John sees, as he had already mentioned in verse 2, the holy city, the new Jerusalem, coming down from heaven and God. Students of Revelation have found this section of Revelation difficult to understand and so there have been several guesses as to the meaning. Some do not want to accept a literal interpretation; some want to consider this a reflection back to the millennium period; others want to consider that this city was suspended above the earth during the millennium and was a dwelling for resurrected saints. I find most of these interpretations to be unacceptable. It seems that a literal interpretation is the best if God does not indicate that it is meant to be a symbolic description and gives us no alternative meaning to this passage. We must, however, consider all of the information He does provide.

The angel's first comment is that he will show John the bride, the wife of the Lamb, but John sees a beautiful city descending to earth, having the glory of God and a brilliance like a costly stone. The bride, who is now also referred to as the wife of the Lamb and rightly so after being married a thousand years, is undoubtedly an occupant of the city. Verse 22 indicates that the Lord God and the Lamb are its temple, consequently they are both occupants and the bride will certainly be with her husband.

John then gives us a great description of the beauty of the city and the layout, but says very little regarding its occupants. There are twelve gates, one for each of the twelve tribes of Israel, and twelve foundation stones to the city, one for each of the apostles of the Lamb. The tribes represent the nation of Israel, who is the wife of God (Jeremiah 31:32), His chosen people, and the beneficiaries of His promises and covenants. The Apostles represent those believers in and followers of Christ through whose sacrificial death and resurrection salvation was obtained for all who believe. We must refer to Hebrews for a list of the occupants of the new Jerusalem. There were myriads of angels, the general assembly (probably those Israelites from ages past who were seen as souls under the altar in Revelation 6 and whose faith was counted as righteousness), the church of the first-born (the church as we know it), God, the spirits of righteous men made perfect (those not included elsewhere such as tribulation martyrs and those from the millennium), and Jesus (Hebrews 12:22-24).

John then gives the dimensions of the city. It is laid out as a square and is measured by the angel with a gold measuring rod. The city is long as it is wide, measuring approximately fifteen hundred miles in each direction. An area this large would extend from New York to the middle of Kansas and from the Canadian border to the Gulf of Mexico (or about half the size of the United States). It is also fifteen hundred miles high, which seems strange. This sounds like a science fiction city that we see in movies where people move around in various kinds of transportation, such as small personal futuristic aircraft and suspended roadways or railways. I suppose that sort of imaging is possible after the Lord's thousand-year reign of peace, which should bring amazing discoveries and creations if man is allowed to continue his scientific research and progress. A more probable explanation may have something to do with the angels and other heavenly beings that God and the Lamb have serving them; the height of this city will accommodate them. There is no indication as to how much space they will occupy nor what kind of facilities they will require. I believe there are many things that we cannot even come close to visualizing, so it would be quite presumptuous to attempt to base guesses upon our finite visualization of future needs or to say we should not accept a literal interpretation of these passages simply because we cannot imagine it.

Verses 18-23

These verses describe the precious stones and metals that constitute the various parts of the city's construction. They are provided in such detail that it appears there may be symbolic meaning in them; however, if there is, the passage does not provide clues as to what they might be.

John seems rather surprised, as he comments in verse 22, that he sees no temple in the city. His commission is to report what he sees and not what he doesn't see. He was, of course, a Christian and had undoubtedly discontinued the Jewish worship traditions, but temple worship had been such a part of his life and environment that it was the first thing he looked for. He comments that the Lord God, the Almighty, and Lamb are its temple. I assume this means that a house of worship is no longer needed to worship God and the Lamb, for they may be worshiped directly. In fact, it seems that the whole city is a temple since it is the home of God and the Lamb. John also indicates that the glory of God illumines the city and the Lamb is the lamp, so there is no need for the sun or the moon. It is interesting that he does not mention the other major function of the sun, which is to provide heat; however, as mentioned in Hebrews 12:29. "Our God is a consuming fire," so He will be the source of heat, assuming there is a need for it, just as He is light.

Verses 24-27

John discusses how the nations will walk by the light of the city and will bring their glory and honor into it. The kings of the earth will bring their glory into the city, and the gates will never be closed for it will always be daylight. He closes by saying that "nothing unclean and no one who practices abomination and lying, shall ever come into it, but only those whose names are written in the Lamb's book of life."

These are puzzling statements for John speaks as though there will be evil inhabitants outside the city, and although they have access to the city, they are kept out. It sounds as if some of these inhabitants and nations will be welcome in the city for they will be of appropriate righteousness, while others will not be allowed in. I have no explanation for these comments for my understanding is that at the creation of the new heaven and new earth, all of those judged unrighteous in the great white throne judgments, as well as Satan, will be in the lake of fire; the only ones left are the righteous who will all be in the new Jerusalem. Scripture give us no clue as to whether these remarks are to be interpreted other than literally, so I will leave them to your judgment and imagination, with my only comment being that it does appear that there will be activity outside the city. There will be a new earth, and if it is the size of our present earth, it would make sense that the part not used as a foundation for the new Jerusalem would be used in some manner, possibly in activities such as farming and manufacturing as support for the huge city of new Jerusalem.

REVELATION 22

Verses 1-2

John continues his observations regarding this beautiful city that has descended from God to earth. He sees a river of the water of life coming from the throne of God and the Lamb down the middle of its street. (I assume "its street" refers to the main street of the city, so the river must run fifteen hundred miles.) John refers to one throne for both God and the Lamb, which must imply that the Lamb is sitting at the Father's right hand. This would be as Christ answered the high priest when asked if He were the Son of God: "You have said it yourself; nevertheless I tell you, hereafter you shall see THE SON OF MAN SITTING AT THE RIGHT HAND OF POWER, AND COMING ON THE CLOUDS OF HEAVEN" (Matthew 26:64).

John also speaks of the tree of life as being on either side of the river and bearing a different kind of fruit each month of the year. One commentator believes it appears to be on both sides of the river because the river is narrow and the tree is large and draping over the river. A rather minor point. It is more interesting to trace the available history of the tree of life. It is first mentioned in Genesis 2:9 and 3:22 as being in the Garden of Eden and was one of the reasons God removed Adam and Eve from the Garden after they sinned. God said they had to be expelled because they might eat from the tree "and live forever" (Genesis 3:22). Then, according to verse 24, God placed the cherubim and a flaming sword to guard the way to the tree of life. Apparently God did not destroy the Garden or the tree of life which were located on the earth at the time of Adam, but established a protective shield that makes them inaccessible and impossible to locate.

In Revelation 2:7 Christ promised to "him who overcomes" the right to "eat of the tree of life, which is in the Paradise of God." This would lead us to the conclusion that the Garden and Paradise are possibly the same. We are then reminded that Christ promised the thief on the cross that he would be with Him that very day in Paradise (Luke 23:43). This seems to lead to the possibility that the Garden or Paradise may be the intermediate heaven where those who die in the faith spend time with Jesus awaiting the resurrection at the rapture. These various passages do not confirm the location of the tree, the Garden or Paradise, but since the tree of life is described as being in both, it does raise the possibility that they are one and the same, and assuming God did not destroy the Garden, then they are probably on the earth. In the final reference referring to the tree (Revelation 22:2), it is said to be in the new Jerusalem. It appears to be fairly certain that the old earth and heaven have been replaced. If the garden and tree were hidden on the old earth, they will either be replaced or they will be moved to a new location in the new Jerusalem.

Another characteristic of the tree of life, mentioned by John, is the use of its leaves to heal the nations. This is, once again, a puzzling statement that most commentators cannot explain. I believe that it follows the earlier statements that there is some activity outside the new Jerusalem that is not clear in Scripture. The healing power of the tree may be necessary and used by the nations to allow them to enter the city and bring their glory with them (21:26).

Verses 3-5

Verses 3 through 5 further describe the city, some of which John felt it was necessary to repeat. There shall no longer be any curse. The throne of God and the Lamb shall be in it (as mentioned in chapter 21), and His bond-servants shall serve Him. Note that although the throne is described to be of both God and the Lamb, when it mentions the service of the bond-servants it says they "shall serve Him." It appears that, as mentioned earlier, the Lamb has placed all things under the Father and as it says in 1 Corinthians 15:28, "When all things are subjected to Him, then the Son Himself also will be subjected to the One who subjected all things to Him, that God may be all in all."

The bondservants will be privileged to see His (again singular) face and His name will be on their foreheads. This promise was made to the church at Philadelphia in 3:12, "He who overcomes…I will write upon him the name of My God, and the name of the city of My God, the new Jerusalem, which comes down out of heaven from My God, and My new name." Then in verse 5 John repeats what he had written in 21:25, "And there shall no longer be any night," as the Lord God will provide the illumination.

Verses 6-13

The angel confirmed to John "These words are faithful and true" and repeated the affirmation from 1:1 that God sent His angel to show His bond-servants the things which must shortly take place.

Verse 7 begins the closing summary of Christ's message through John to His bondservants. "And behold, I am coming quickly. Blessed is he who heeds the words of the prophecy of this book." Here, as the book comes to a close, Christ repeats two vital messages: a warning for the third time in Revelation that He is coming quickly. And He again repeats a blessing, the sixth beatitude in Revelation, similar to that made in the opening segment in 1:3, that he who heeds the words of the prophecy in this book will be blessed.

John confirms, in verse 8, that he is the one who heard and saw the things recorded in Revelation. He, again, makes the mistake of attempting to worship the angel that had been his guide and is told not to do that for the angel is a fellow servant. John should worship God alone.

He is then told, "Do not seal up the words of the prophecy of this book, for the time is near." This is a different message than the angel gave to Daniel, for Daniel had been told to seal up the words of his book (Daniel 12:4). As I commented in my remarks on Daniel, I believe that Revelation is an elaboration, from 6:1–22:7 of the book that Daniel was told to close "until the end of time."

Verse 11 is a statement that says it will be too late to change after the Lord comes, so he who does wrong, and he who is filthy, and the one who is right, and the one who is holy, each will continue in his particular lifestyle. In other words, life will go on as it always has until Jesus comes. In verse 12, He repeats, "I am coming quickly, and My reward is with Me, to render to every man according to what he has done." This apparently is in reference to the judgment seat of Christ before which all Christians must appear and their deeds judged for purposes of administering the reward as mentioned in 2 Corinthians 5:10. He confirms that He is "the Alpha and the Omega, the first and the last, the beginning and the end," repeating His declarations in 1:8 and 21:6.

Verses 14-15

Verses 14 and 15 begin with a beatitude, the seventh one in Revelation, blessing everyone "who wash their robes, that they may have the right to the tree of life, and may enter by the gates into the city." I presume the washing is intended to be in the blood of the Lamb, as did those in 7:14.

He then indicates that outside are dogs, sorcerers, immoral persons, murderers, idolaters, and liars. As in chapter 21, some of the descriptive remarks sound as if there will be activities outside the city. Some will be conducted by righteous people, for they may enter the gates and have a right to the tree of life. The immoral ones outside the city are not allowed to enter (21:27). I assume that He would have made it clear if He were referring to those who were sentenced to the lake of fire. As noted in chapter 21, most commentators do not expect activity outside the new Jerusalem and either ignore the implications of the remarks or explain them away as referring to those who receive rewards and those who do not. Taking this literally, I believe that there will be people living outside the city carrying on daily life as we do now. I do not understand it, but I believe God's Word implies it.

Verses 16-21

In these verses, Christ makes it clear that He is the one who sent an angel to testify these things for the churches. He is from David's line making Him the heir of David's throne and the One who fulfills the promises of the Davidic covenant He is the bright morning star of prophecy, portending a bright new day with the new heaven and earth. This reference is the first time that the church has been mentioned since chapter 3. Christ extends that wonderful invitation to all generations to "come." Those who are thirsty and those who wish to drink from the water of life can come without cost. The invitation is from the Holy Spirit, the bride (the church), and those who hear and pass on the invitation to come.

Verses 18 and 19 hold a serious warning to those who might want to interpret the book in their own words and under their own terms. Christ (the "I" in verse 18 must be Christ for He is the only one who can commit the Father to the judgments promised) testifies to everyone who hears the words of this prophecy that anyone who adds to the words of this book will suffer the plagues written in this book, and anyone who takes away from the book will lose his part in the tree of life and the holy city. I believe the "add to" and "take away" warnings are not meant to discourage earnest attempts to interpret the Holy Spirit's meaning and purpose, but to discourage any use of interpretation to promote personal agendas. He who testifies these things says, "Yes, I am coming quickly." Amen. Come Lord Jesus. The grace of the Lord Jesus be with all. Amen.